0044712838

7/01

Gaines, Ann

The composite
guide to extreme
sports

DUE DATE   0201   16.95

4001428
5542 4848

000 030   000 013

IN THIS SERIES

Auto Racing

Baseball

Basketball

Bodybuilding

Extreme Sports

Field Hockey

Figure Skating

Football

Golf

Gymnastics

Hockey

Lacrosse

Martial Arts

Soccer

Softball

Strongman Competition

Tennis

Track and Field

Volleyball

Wrestling

THE COMPOSITE GUIDE

to **EXTREME SPORTS**

ANN GRAHAM GAINES

CHELSEA HOUSE PUBLISHERS
Philadelphia

Produced by Choptank Syndicate, Inc. and Chestnut Productions

Senior Editor: Norman L. Macht
Editor and Picture Researcher: Mary E. Hull
Design and Production: Lisa Hochstein
Cover Illustrator: Cliff Spohn

Project Editor: Jim McAvoy
Art Direction: Sara Davis
Cover Design: Keith Trego

First Printing

1 3 5 7 9 8 6 4 2

Library of Congress Cataloging-in-Publication Data

Gaines, Ann.
      The composite guide to extreme sports / by Ann Graham Gaines.
            p.   cm.—(The composite guide)
      Includes bibliographical references (p. 62).
      Summary: Surveys the history, equipment, and techniques of such extreme sports as sky
surfing, mountain climbing, roller blading, and skateboarding and describes the X-Games,
created to celebrate them.
      ISBN 0-7910-5862-X
      1. Extreme Sports—Juvenile literature. 2. ESPN X-Games—Juvenile literature.
[1. Extreme sports.] 1. Title. II. Series.
GV749.7. G25 2000

                                                                99-087374

CONTENTS

1

SKY SURFING

Over 250,000 people gathered to watch dangerous and exciting new sports at the X Games in San Francisco, California, in the summer of 1999. Although these spectators watched bikers go end-over-end with their bicycles in double somersaults and street lugers hurtling down the San Francisco hills at speeds close to 70 mph, lying flat on their backs only a couple of inches from the ground, not even the judges really saw what happened thousands of feet above the city in what is perhaps the most exciting sport of all, sky surfing.

In order to judge the competitors in this sport, the judges put a videotape into a VCR. They watched one sky dancer standing on a small surfboard, photographed from only a few feet away by his partner, as both of them jumped from an airplane and fell at 140 mph from 10,500 feet. The surfer danced in the air, turned upside down, made the board into a helicopter rotor, and did cartwheels and gymnastic tumbles. Surfing through the clouds, he looked like the "Silver Surfer" in the Marvel comic books of years ago. When the two sky surfers reached 5,000 feet, they deployed their parachutes and expertly touched down at the landing site.

Parachute jumpers started sky surfing in southern California in the early 1980s when they began to jump with a Styrofoam boogie

Wearing a camera on his head, Rickster Powell, left, films his partner, Viviane Wegrath of Switzerland, as she sky surfs over the southern Swiss city of Lugano during the "Boards over Europe" sky surfing competition held in August 1997.

Olive Furrer, left, and his cameraman, Christian Schmidt, won the "Boards over Europe" sky surfing competition in 1997 by falling from the greatest height—4,000 meters.

board designed for bodysurfing in the ocean. The jumpers would lie flat on the board and try to steer it through the air as they fell. They called it "air surfing." In 1986, Joel Schlively and Mike Deluna were filmed by Dave Detell on boogie boards as all three fell through the air for a television news program. In France in 1987, Joel Cruciani screwed ski boots onto a board and became the first person to stand on a freely falling board, as if he were riding a giant wave. Later, Cruciani, a stunt man and expert sky diver, repeated this feat for the film *Hibernator* using a standard-sized surfboard

equipped with snowboard boot bindings. This film helped popularize the sport, which quickly attracted newcomers seeking the "rush" or thrill that comes from falling freely through the air before the parachute opens. Sky surfers quickly added such safety features as soft bindings and a cutaway system to the board. They also attached a separate parachute to the board itself in case an emergency made the sky surfer abandon it.

In the fall of 1990, the first Sky Surfing World Freestyle Championship took place. But there was no way to judge the jumps from the ground, even with high-powered binoculars. It was necessary for a cameraman to jump alongside the surfer and videotape the jump, which could then be viewed by the judges. Thus sky surfing became a team sport, since the two jumpers had to fall together and stay in sync for the tricks of the jump to be recorded properly.

The pioneers in the sport of sky surfing were forced to make it up as they went along. For a long time, there were no instruction manuals to read or schools to attend to learn how to sky surf. The sport has grown so popular that manuals are now available, and just flipping through them is enough to keep most people at a safe distance from this extremely dangerous sport. Sky surfers must be expert parachute jumpers who have already made hundreds of jumps and reached a point where they feel relaxed falling through the air. It takes over 50 practice jumps to learn how to stand up in a stable position while falling from 9,500 to 3,500 feet. Next, the new sky surfer must learn how to start and stop 360-degree flat spins. Then a sky surfer must practice spinning 360 degrees in one direction, stopping, and spinning 360 degrees in the other direction. Learning all of this might take another 100 jumps, as well as hundreds of hours of practice on the ground before the sky surfer ever gets to jump with a sky board.

The tricks of sky surfing are incredibly difficult to master. For example, here are the instructions to perform a simple trick, as explained in the article "Sky Surfing" on the website

www.koyn.com/CloudDancer/articles/Surf.html:

To bring the sky board under you from the inverted orientation, your goal is to "knife" the edge of the sky board into the wind. The sky board presents much less drag when its edge is presented into the wind flow. (The sky board catches much more wind if one of its flat sides is presented to the wind flow.) It is easier to knife the sky board under yourself with a sideways rotation. While trying to bring it forward or backward while knifing it into the wind, the sky surfer must accommodate the long length of the board. You will be fighting the tail of the sky board if you are bringing it under yourself from a rocking front loop action and you will be fighting the nose of the sky board if you are bringing it under yourself from a rocking back loop action. A cartwheel action is the best rotational movement for bringing the sky board back under yourself. If it is a left cartwheel with the left foot forward, your chest will twist to the right as you stand up again. Relaxing the legs as you pass side into the wind position will allow the sky board to find the optimum knife edge presentation to the wind.

Sky surfing tricks are not only difficult to learn, they are extremely dangerous. All sky surfing takes place at over 100 mph, as the surfer's body hurtles toward the ground below. If the surfer cannot control the board, he or she must turn into the vertical head-down position and release the board. Releasing the board while standing may cause it to fly up, resulting in severe injuries to the head or other body parts. Blacking out is a hazard that may follow an uncontrolled spin, and just before blacking out a sky surfer may experience red spots in his or her vision. If either foot comes loose from the board or the bindings break, the board must be released immediately, to prevent it from flying up and breaking a surfer's leg.

Sky surfing is one of many extreme sports created in the latter part of the 20th century. These new sports often took advantage of new developments in technology, using equipment like polyurethane wheels, fiberglass boards, and titanium bike frames that were unavailable just a few years earlier.

2 THE X GAMES

In 1995, the television network ESPN started a new kind of Olympic Games in Newport, Rhode Island, called the X Games. These games featured sports that used the latest equipment, including BMX bicycles, in-line roller skates, and three or four varieties of skateboards, snowboards, and wakeboards.

The X in the X Games stood for extreme. What made these new extreme sports alike, besides their use of 20th century technology, was the daring and courage they demanded—they put the participant on the edge of physical danger. Serious injuries rarely occur in track and field events, for example, but sky surfing and street luging accidents can be fatal. Extreme sports attract people who are eager for the thrill of living dangerously. From the beginning, the X Games attracted a different kind of athlete. Many of them had tattoos, and some wore rings through their noses. When a television cameraman asked an in-line skater to remove his baseball hat, hold up a tag with his name on it, and look into the camera for a close-up, he displayed a typical attitude, shaking his head in disgust. As he turned away, he simply said, "Too many rules, dude."

The X Games had few organized rules. In fact, some of the sports chosen for inclusion in the original X Games of 1995 did not even have an official name. Bungee jumping, a five-day

Klas Vangen of Norway flies in the air during a training run in the snowboard halfpipe in Yamanouchi, Japan, where he competed in the 1998 winter Olympics. Snowboarding is one X Games sport that is also an Olympic competition.

To accommodate snow-boarding competition at the 1997 X Games in San Diego, ESPN built a ramp and covered it with 200 tons of artificial snow. Jason Borgestede of Alaska, shown airborne, took third place at the Men's Snowboarding Big Air event on June 28, 1997.

marathon called an eco-challenge, sport climbing, bicycle stunts, barefoot jumping, street luge, aggressive and downhill in-line skating, skateboarding, and sky surfing were first chosen as events. Some of these quickly disappeared from the games. Bungee jumping was eliminated from the 1997 event when there was no way found to judge it. The eco-challenge was eliminated in 1996. All a television camera could record was the start and the finish, as the rest of the event took place in the wilderness. The X Games were created for TV audiences, and the producers wanted to keep the games interesting to the viewing public. In order to do so, ESPN used more than 100 television cameras to cover the events. They placed a tiny radio frequency television camera in the handle of a barefoot jumper's tow rope in the water skiing event and put a digital camera in the helmet of the ESPN cameraman who jumped alongside the sky surfing team to catch the teamwork between the surfer and his cameraman as they fell.

In 1997 ESPN moved the summer games to San Diego, California, and announced it would sponsor a second series of X Games featuring the winter extreme sports. In order to preview these new games, ESPN decided to demonstrate one of the most spectacular winter sports—big air snowboarding—at the summer games in San Diego. Big air snow requires a snow-topped mountain with a downhill slide that allows skiers to get up enough speed for gymnastic tricks. There are no snow-topped mountains in San Diego. So ESPN decided to create one. First they built a ramp, 250 feet long and 90 feet high, from eight truckloads of scaffolding and 50,000 pounds of cement. Then they made snow using 60,000 gallons of liquid nitrogen at a temperature of -320 degrees Fahrenheit to turn 60,000 gallons of water into instant snow pumped through hoses onto the ramp. The night before the competition, workers put down a base layer and covered it with an insulating blanket. The next morning another foot of instant snow was created. There in the middle of the summer sat 200 tons of snow. Peter Line won the men's and Tina Dixon captured the women's snowboarding competition, but it was the glistening white powder itself that was the star.

That summer in San Diego athletes from around the globe competed in 28 events in nine categories: aggressive in-line skating, big air snowboarding, bicycle stunt, downhill in-line skating, skateboarding, sky surfing, sport climbing, street luge, and water sports. According to ESPN, 220,000 spectators attended the X Games, and 14 million households worldwide tuned in to watch ESPN's and ABC's broadcasts of the events.

The first winter X Games were held in the winter of 1997 at the Snow Summit Resort in Big Bear Lake, California. They featured events in four categories, including ice climbing and snow mountain bike racing, in which racers ride specialized bikes down mountain slopes on hardpacked snow, trying to stay upright and score the fastest time. A year later in Crested Butte, Colorado, three new events, including the first motorized event of the games, snowmobile snocross, were added to the winter X Games. The 2000 winter X Games introduced a new sport, UltraCross, which paired skiers and snowboarders in a relay race against time, down a mountain.

ESPN televised the summer and winter X Games events to more than 221 million homes in 190 countries and territories in 20 languages. Over $200,000 were awarded in prizes. The 1998 summer games were attended by a record 242,850 people over the 10 days of competition in San Diego. The 1999 summer games in San Francisco again set a record for attendance when 263,390 spectators showed up. The 2000 winter games held at Mt. Snow, Vermont, were attended by 83,500, the largest number in the 4-year history of winter X. The Mt. Snow ski resort signed a contract with ESPN Sports to host the winter X Games through 2004.

Television is a powerful medium of public awareness, and ESPN's cameras have contributed a great deal to the popularity of extreme sports in the United States. Derek Downing, the winner of the 1995 downhill in-line skating event said, "It's the best thing that ever happened to our sport. No one knew what it was before that—the X Games just put us on the map." In addition to showing the X Games, ESPN began to broadcast many of the various extreme sports as regularly scheduled events throughout the year. Many of the sports formed their own professional organizations to establish rules, rankings, and their own regular competitions.

Tucker Hibbert, 15, of Goodridge, Minnesota, drives his way to victory in the snowmobile snocross competition at the 2000 winter X Games held at the Mt. Snow ski resort in West Dover, Vermont. Snowmobile snocross was introduced to the winter X Games in 1998.

Pete Loncarevich of Orange, California, takes a turn down the mountain in the semifinal round of the men's snow mountain biking competition at the 2000 winter X Games. Sponsored by the ESPN network, the 2000 games boasted the largest attendance in the four-year history of the winter X Games.

Other television networks started their own extreme sports festivals. The Gravity Games were broadcast as two-hour shows on four consecutive Sunday afternoons on the NBC television network in October 1999. These games included new sports like freestyle motocross, as well as live music acts, an extreme sports film festival, and clinics where the recognized pros of the various sports gave interviews and demonstrations.

Dick Ebersol, the head of NBC Sports, said, "We are always looking for exciting new programming concepts. This will be a new vehicle for NBC Sports to expand its young audiences." NBC is not alone in jumping on the economic boom that the new extreme sports present. Mayor Willie L. Brown of San Francisco, who was instrumental in bringing the X Games to his city, wanted to create a permanent local home for the new sports. "You ever heard of the X Games?" Brown asked a reporter from behind his desk. "It's what the young people are in to," said the 64-year-old mayor. "Skateboarding, rock climbing, oddball sports that attract people from all over the world."

Mountain climbing has always been an extreme sport, physically demanding and full of danger. In the middle of the 19th century, Sir Alfred Wills of England published a book that described his ascent of the Wetterhorn, a mountain in the European Alps, and caused mountain climbing to become a popular sport. Women as well as men climbed from the start.

Robyn Erbesfield, ranked first in the World Cup Climbing Championships from 1992–1995, explained, "I'm not big on women's issues so I definitely have never noticed that being a woman is a handicap or a plus. I tend to just [think that] I am a woman and there are men, and we climb together and sometimes I'm stronger, sometimes they're stronger, and basically we just motivate each other."

In 1871 Lucy Walker was the first woman to climb the Matterhorn, the 14,688-foot Alpine peak at the border of Italy and Switzerland. American climbers Fanny Bullock and Annie Peck made many climbs early in the 20th century. Peck climbed the 21,838-foot South American Andean peak of Huascaran in 1908 when she was 58 years old. Between 1911 and 1944, a Frenchwoman, Alexandra David-Neel, traveled alone to Tibet disguised as a beggar and made several high altitude ascents of Himalayan mountains. In 1934 Hettie Dyhrenfurth climbed the 24,371-foot Queen Mary peak in Kasmir,

Climbing specialist Lisa Rust of Hood River, Oregon, climbs the façade of 25 Broadway in New York City on November 2, 1999, while filming a commercial for the online store PlanetOutdoors.com.

Pakistan. In 1974, three Japanese women climbed the Nepalese peak of Manaslu, which reaches 26,750 feet. Traditionally, climbing has been a solo or a team accomplishment, but in the 1980s, with the invention of free climbing and competition climbing, it became a competition event and an extreme sport.

From the beginning of mountain climbing, climbers used ropes and other devices to help them up the mountain face and to protect them from falling. Large iron spikes, called pitons, were driven into the cracks on a rock face. Climbers could stand on these or secure safety ropes to them. Climbers left these pitons embedded into the rock as they moved on. Over the years, many famous climbs became cluttered with pitons. They not only looked ugly, but they often widened cracks in the rock face and made climbs more difficult and dangerous.

In the middle of the 20th century, climbers began to free climb—climb unaided, using only a safety rope in case they fell. It was a new sport, requiring more technical and physical skill. It also required more courage.

Lynn Hill of Riverside, California, started free climbing in the 1970s when she was 14 years old. "The first day I went climbing," Hill remembered, "was at Big Rock, a local area near Riverside, California. It's a granite slab, low-angle, a lot of balance and technique. I didn't know anything about the equipment, so when my sister started explaining how to make a Swiss seat for the harness and tying the knots, I was just following along. And then she pointed up, said, 'Okay, now go!' So I did, and I kept climbing and looked down and it seemed kind of strange, but I just kept going.

American climber Fannie Bullock Workman (1859–1925) poses with her mountaineering equipment in 1915. Workman and her husband made detailed maps of the Karakorum region of the Himalayas during their treks. Workman, who continued to climb in the Himalayas into her late fifties, was known for once carrying a "Votes for Women" banner with her on expedition.

And at the end of the climb she said, 'Okay, that's the top, now you can come down.' I thought, 'oooh, you know, this is intense!' But I didn't really even know if it was dangerous or not . . . I guess you could say I had a pretty unusual introduction to climbing. But I was always a good athlete as a kid. . . . So I was used to actually doing things and going for it, you know. Or trying new things. And I probably didn't understand the risks, either, but since I'd never had a problem with it, I learned that if you focus on what you're doing and try hard, usually it works out."

Over the next two decades Hill led her sport of women's free climbing into the mainstream.

This 1885 illustration shows a female mountaineer in Victorian dress turning a corner in the Austrian Alps with the help of guides and ropes.

In 1979 she made the first ascent of Ophir Broke, a climb in Colorado which, at the time, ranked as the hardest route ever followed by a woman. She scored in every sport climbing competition that she entered in the '80s. In 1992, Hill became the first woman to free climb "the Nose," taking the most popular route up El Capitan, the completely vertical granite face in Yosemite National Park. The next year, she did it in a day. She has become an inspiration to all climbers, male and female. Hill did not let success spoil her enjoyment of the sport. "One of the things that's intriguing about climbing is discovery. Personal discovery as well as in the environment. What I like doing is going to places that I've never been, and being with nice people, certainly beautiful places, and rock climbing. That's the thing that I like the most, rock climbing."

Competition climbing developed from the sport of free climbing. At first the competitions took place outdoors on an actual cliff face. Climbers would see who was the fastest or who had the most style going up a boulder or rock face. But quite soon the competitions moved inside to artificial mountains built onto the sides of walls, offering routes of varying difficulty. Originally a "rock gym," the name for an indoor wall used to practice holds and climbing maneuvers, was only for training—a place to practice during the winter months when it was impossible to climb outside. Today, indoor climbing has become a sport in itself. Rock gyms are located mostly in large cities. People like them because they require little equipment and are quite safe, yet also challenging.

The holds of an artificial wall are usually man-made pieces attached to the wall by bolts. They come in all sizes and shapes and have a variety of colorful names such as "chickenhead" for a round hold that sticks out from the wall or "crimper" for a small hold just big enough for the fingertips to grip.

There are two kinds of competition climbing: speed climbing and difficulty climbing. In speed climbing two climbers race side by side up two identical courses to see who gets to the top first. The climbers in the difficulty competition each make one attempt in a certain amount of time to scale the top of a preset route. The route remains unknown to the climber until five minutes prior to the competition. In both speed and difficulty climbing, competitors wear a safety harness and ropes to prevent serious injuries. They also wear climbing shoes that resemble tight ballet slippers, and they carry a bag holding chalk they can use to keep their hands dry during the climb.

Major world climbing competitions include the Cerre Chevalier in France, the Arco in Italy, and the Extreme Games in the United States, each with several divisions for young climbers.

Lynn Hill was one of the first stars of competition climbing, but she soon retired from active competition and returned to rock climbing. Into Lynn's spot stepped tiny Katie Brown from Georgia, who at an even five feet and 85 pounds has one of the greatest

Sixteen-year-old Katie Brown of Lafayette, Georgia, works her way up the overhanging climbing wall during the finals of the women's climbing difficulty competition at the 1997 X Games in San Diego. Brown won the contest.

strength-to- body weight ratios of any climber. Katie started climbing in 1993 at the age of 13. Her mother, Eileen, a climber herself, introduced the teenager to the sport. Two years later, Katie won her age group at the Junior Nationals, and a few months after that, she won fourth place at the Senior Nationals. Her mother commented on her astounding progress. "She doesn't realize how good she is, and I don't think she wants to realize it. When she started climbing, I don't think she could've imagined it would lead to this."

In March 1996 Katie won her first adult competition against Mia Axon, one of the world's premier free climbers. At the X Games in Newport, Rhode Island, that year Katie was the last competitor in her event to try the difficult course. Each of the other seven competitors had fallen short of the top of the 42-foot wall. Katie calmly kept going up, fitting her tiny hands perfectly onto each hold. When the announcement was made that only 60 seconds remained in her climb, Katie pushed past the super-difficult place where the other climbers had fallen and sprang to the top, grabbing the final hold. As she was lowered to the bottom, she broke into a smile and waved to the cheering crowd below. Katie, who was too young to have a driver's license, had a harder time with the television and newspaper reporters who crowded around her than she did with the climb. Her answers were short and to the point. Most of the time she nervously played with the large gold medal she was wearing around her neck.

At the 1997 X Games in San Diego, California, it was much the same story. Katie scaled the 54-foot wall with an ease that astonished the cheering audience. The next year, Katie was the only one to finish the 60-foot climb. All of the other seven competitors had fallen. Three of the competitors had come within one hold of the top, but their approach to the final hold had left their bodies in such an awkward position that the final few inches were impossible. Katie had also fallen from this route in the semifinals, but in her final effort she changed the way she approached several challenging moves and made the final lunge to the top with ease.

4 SKATING

In 1760 Joseph Merlin wanted to be able to ice-skate when there was no snow or ice. He attached wooden spools to the soles of his shoes, but discovered he could not turn or stop. In addition, there were no paved roads for him to skate on. His idea was soon forgotten.

In the early 1800s, Robert John Tyers of London, England, another ice-skater who wanted to skate in warm weather, put five wheels in a line on each of his shoes. This invention, which Tyers called the "rolito," worked well enough, but it never became popular.

In 1863, in New York, James L. Plimpton created what we recognize as traditional roller skates, with two wheels mounted together at the toe of the shoe and two other wheels mounted at the heel. This design was much more stable and easier to use than the earliest in-line skates. As the streets and sidewalks of the cities became paved in the beginning of the 20th century, roller-skating became a popular pastime for kids and grown-ups alike.

In 1980, two brothers in Minnesota, Scott and Brennan Olson, designed new in-line skates for hockey players who wanted to practice in the warm weather months. They called their skates roller blades and made them in the basement of their parents' home. The new "blades" became popular not only with practicing hockey players and skiers but with those who also enjoyed the

Idaho's Eric Bailey soars upside down during the street course in-line skating event at the Panasonic Shock-Wave U.S. Open of in-line skating, held in Huntington Beach, California, in July 1999.

old-style roller skates. The new skates were so much faster that they cut minutes, not seconds, from speed records.

In-line skates are built like ski-boots on wheels. Each skate starts with a hard plastic or leather outer shell that is joined to a hard plastic or aluminum frame on the bottom that holds the wheels. There is a softer inner liner of leather or cloth that molds to the foot and feels like a soft boot. The hard outer shell supports the ankle and makes using the skates easier and more fun. The wheels—there can be three, four, or five on each skate—come in different sizes. The larger the wheel, the faster the skate can go. The wheels also come in harder and softer materials. Harder wheels increase speed; softer wheels dig into the ground better and allow faster acceleration and stopping. Skaters can easily go 25 miles an hour on level ground. Downhill racers reach 55 miles an hour.

Smart racers always wear a helmet to protect their heads if they should fall. Besides a helmet, racers wear shin, knee, and elbow protectors. In 1984, there were 20,000 in-line skaters in America. By 1994, there were 12 million worldwide.

Skaters have their own magazine, *Inline Magazine*, devoted to the more radical aspects of the sport. Skates are used regularly for exercise, dancing, races, street-hockey games, and many other sports. The X Games include aggressive skating, or trick skating, events that are conducted on both the half pipe and on courses designed to look like a city landscape or the inside of a shopping mall without the pedestrians but with handrails, concrete benches, and ramps. Races include one event created especially for the X Games—the down-hill races—a lengthy run that features many difficult twists and turns.

In the downhill race, each contestant makes two solo downhill runs to determine his best time. The best times in the qualifying runs get the best positions at the top of the hill. The two best finishers in each preliminary heat advance to the next level of races. Judges watch for fouls such as tripping and holding. One final race determines the winner. Spandex-clad racers draft each other on the way down at speeds over 50 mph as they aim for a place to pass or rocket ahead of the others. There is quite an advantage gained in drafting the lead racer, so, as with Olympic bicycle races, no one jumps to the front on the start; the racers go slow on purpose until one of them, trying to take the others by surprise, sprints ahead. The others quickly follow and the all-out race is on. Winners must cross the finish line with the wheels of their lead skate on the ground.

Downhill skating can be dangerous. In 1996 defending champion Derek Downing broke his collarbone in five places.

Women's races were added to the X Games in 1996, and Gypsy Tidwell from Waco, Texas, who was the fastest woman on flat land courses in 1994, won the event.

For years, the sport of trick skating was looked down upon by the general public. Almost the only times that the average citizen would see the aggressive skaters would be while they were walking on the streets or strolling the shopping malls of their suburban neighborhoods. Onlookers often saw only the

Patented around 1880, these wooden roller skates with leather bindings were supposed to allow greater freedom of movement than earlier versions. Roller-skating was so popular in the U.S. during the 1870s and 1880s that roller rinks were constructed in almost every city.

In-line skater Raphael Sandoz of Switzerland flies through the air during the men's half-pipe vertical finals at the 1996 X Games in Newport, Rhode Island. Sandoz finished sixth in the event.

tattoos and baggy pants of the skaters and completely missed the difficulty and beauty of the moves. The sport got its first positive national exposure on prime-time TV in the X Games, where the beauty and daring of all the extreme sports was displayed. The Aggressive Skaters Association (ASA) was formed in 1995 in order to create and promote a professional sport of skating.

In 1996 the new pro skaters teamed up with bikers and skateboarders to produce a national tour of the extreme sports and give everyone around the country an up-close look at these new sports. The best of the skaters received publicity and product endorsements. The ASA set up a professional circuit of events that were regularly shown on ESPN throughout the year.

In both the vert (half-pipe) and the street contests, skaters are given about a minute to complete each of two preliminary runs. Seven judges rate the performance on style, difficulty, consistency, and line. The scores of the runs are averaged and determine the final order of the top qualifiers. In the finals, each contestant is given three chances. Their lowest score is thrown out, the other two averaged, and the top score signals the winner. If there is a tie for the winner, they have a run-off.

In 1997, the ASA formed another organization for the amateur skater and began to schedule events only for them. "Before it was who you knew," said Todd Shays, executive director of ASA, "now it clearly has more to do with how you do in competition. Having a performance-based measurement has raised the bar in the competitive world and legitimized the pro class. It's been a wake-up call for the industry and a great way for new skaters to rise in the ranks."

Jason Roy, manager of the Tribe in-line skating team and in-line competition judge, agrees. "The amateur circuit has increased the enthusiasm among skaters, especially the younger ones. Now there's an organized way to find success. The competitive stepping stones go from local contests to regional and on to national. Skaters who can follow that path not only have more competition confidence and experience, but they also know where they stand in the big picture. It's much more clear."

The ASA Pro Tour World Championships and North American Amateur Championships were held in Fort Myers, Florida, in 1999. The events featured the top 30 male professional skaters in both street races and aggressive tricks. The women's events featured the top eight women in comparable events. In addition, the top 100 amateur skaters competed in the North American Amateur Championships to determine the skaters who would qualify for the 2000 Pro Tour.

Skating events in the United States attract young athletes from around the world. Ayumi Kawasaki of Japan, only 12 years old, became the youngest X Games participant ever when she placed third in the women's vert competition in 1997 behind Fabiola de Silva of São

Brazilian in-line skater Fabiola de Silva competes during the final round of the women's aggressive vertical in-line skating competition at the 1997 X Games in San Diego. De Silva won the event.

Paolo, Brazil, a former kickboxer and winner of the 1996 event. At the 1999 summer X Games in San Francisco, Kawasaki won the gold medal in the women's aggressive in-line vert competition. Other gold medal winners included Sayaka Yabe, for the women's aggressive in-line street competition; Nicki Adams, for the men's aggressive in-line street; and Eito Yasutoko, for the men's in-line vert event.

"It's still based on fun and teetering on the edge of craziness," says Todd Shays.

Chris Edwards, looking for something spectacular to begin his vert run in an ASA event in Naples, Florida, jumped from a construction crane used to hold a television camera overlooking the half-pipe for a start.

"We had the crane there for aerial photography, but Chris got it in his head to begin his run from the crane," Shays said. "He stood on the fence inside the basket and flew onto the ramp. You know how Chris is, he almost gets angry with intensity. What was anyone going to do but watch it happen? We knew it was history being made. That's our sport. There's an energy to it that's going to dominate no matter what the structure."

5 SKATEBOARDING

Sometime around 1960, kids in California attached axles and roller skate wheels to the bottoms of tiny fiberglass surfboards. They used their inventions to surf around the parking lots and streets of their neighborhoods. The new sport was an instant success, and by 1964 there were several companies selling skateboards all around the country. *Skateboarder Magazine* started publishing. Soon skateboarders could be seen in shopping malls, parking lots, and on sidewalks and streets.

Skateboarding proved dangerous for both the skateboarders and the members of the general public with whom they occasionally collided. Many towns passed laws outlawing skateboards on paved surfaces.

Then skateboarders discovered that they could use wide cement drainage culverts and empty swimming pools for practice. It was much more difficult to skateboard up and down the sides of a swimming pool than on a flat surface, but it was much more exciting and faster, too. A new sport was born: vertical—or vert—skateboarding.

During the 1970s, new plastic urethane wheels and wider boards made vertical skating easier. In 1977 the Upland Skatepark in Upland, California, opened with a huge, free-form empty swimming pool that gave the best skaters a place to compete. Soon skateparks provided

Mathias Ringstrom of Sweden, top, and Max Dufour of Canada fly in tandem off the vertical ramp during the finals of the skateboarding vert doubles competition at the 1997 X Games in San Diego. In the doubles competition, skateboarders are judged on how well they look together as well as their individual moves.

Thirty-one-year-old Tony Hawk is mobbed by ESPN cameramen as he celebrates with other professional skateboarders after landing a 900-degree rotation on a skateboard from mid-air during the 1999 X Games in San Francisco. The trick had never been accomplished before in the history of skateboarding.

a better and safer place to practice the sport, using plywood ramps called "half-pipes" in honor of the cement drainage culverts they resembled. Skateboarders built a "U" shaped frame from wood and covered it with a skin of plywood sheets, which were covered with Masonite. A piece of PVC pipe was placed at the top of the vertical sides where it met the platform. The skaters used the downside of the ramp for speed and the opposite upside to explode into the air for gymnastic vertical tricks, including somersaults and twists that required the skater to reach down and hold onto the board to keep it from flying off into the crowd.

In 1982 the National Skateboard Association was formed, the skateboarding magazine

Thrasher began publication, and a 14-year-old named Tony Hawk won the first all-California skateboarding competition at Delmar State Ranch.

Tony began boarding at the age of 10 with the full support of both his parents and his older brother, Steve. "Actually, my Dad was always supportive of whatever we wanted to do, and so when I was into baseball, he was the coach and he was a lot of help. And I finally told him I wanted to quit—it was just coincidence that they had appointed him president [of the league]. And he still did it, but he still supported my skating as well. He drove me to the skate park almost every day, or every time I went." It didn't cost a lot of money to get into skateboarding in the beginning. "Back in the late '70s when I started, the boards were so cheaply made that it was hard to find a good board. I think I started out with just a generic skateboard," Tony said. Later, a good board made from seven-ply maple with two trick metal trucks and four polyurethane wheels attached underneath could cost $150.

Seventeen years later, Tony Hawk had become the most dominant athlete in all of the extreme competitive sports. Named Skateboarder of the Decade for the 1980s by *Thrasher* magazine, he had won three gold and two silver medals in vertical trick competition. "My inspiration at the beginning of my career was to put skateboarding on the map. That was what drove me, to get skating recognized. Now that we do get a lot more recognition, I just skate for fun now."

Tony never complained about hard work, pain, and a lot of boring practice. It all resulted in the development of one of his proudest feats, which he called a "kickflip McTwist." It's a 540-degree rotation while flipping the board one time. At 8:32 p.m. on June 27, 1999, he added an even harder trick to his list of spectacular moves. In the chilly air of San Francisco he became the first person to successfully complete a 900-degree turn while skating the half-pipe. After 10 attempts had failed in competition, he finally hit it while going for the gold medal. Practice, practice, practice was the key to Tony's success, "I've said this to a couple of others already, but it's all practice. . . . I get my creativity from just constant practice. I am always trying new things on the ramp. It just comes to me. I'll be up in the air and I'll just try something new. If I think it will work, then I'll keep practicing it."

Tony Hawk achieved more public exposure as a professional athlete and as director of his own skateboard company. He has also appeared in television commercials and worked as a stunt double in the movie *Escape from L.A.* His other film credits include *Gleaming the Cube, Police Academy 4: Citizens on Patrol*, and *Fleshwound 2.* He helped design a skateboarding video game, *Tony Hawk's Pro Skater.*

Along the way, Tony got married to his in-line skating sweetheart, Erin. They soon became the parents of two sons, Riley and Spencer. Riley became a skateboarder and often practiced with his dad. "Kid's not scared of anything," said Tony. "We go to the skate park and we're there for a couple hours and sometimes he wants to stay longer than I do. . . . He's so determined to do the things he wants to do that he'll do them at almost any

cost. Even if he's getting hurt along the way, it doesn't stop him and that's really how I was."

In the 1997 X Games, Tony Hawk and Andy Macdonald, who had beaten out Hawk in the 1996 and 1998 vert competition for the gold medal, combined in a new event, the doubles competition. They were judged not only for the skills of their individual moves but for how they looked together. Hawk and Macdonald easily took home the gold. In 1998, they again teamed up in the doubles competition. On their final run, which earned a 96.0 from the amazed judges, Andy did a front side method air while flying over Tony's 540-degree twist below him. They were tumbling so close together that they collided. Andy later

Andy Macdonald, one of the world's top skateboarders, competes in the 1999 X Games in San Francisco, California. Macdonald teamed with Tony Hawk in the doubles competition at the 1997 and 1998 X Games, where the two amazed judges with their daring routines.

Chris Senn of Costa Mesa, California, soars above the fans as he competes in the skateboarding street finals at the 1996 X Games in Newport, Rhode Island. Senn finished second in the event.

explained, "On that last run, I was a bit too close, I put my hand on his back to make sure I was by him. That made Tony nervous, because he doesn't know what's going on behind him."

Tony said, "I figured once he hit me, he was falling. And then I look over and he's still going. So I figured it was still on. We pretty much had our routine dialed. We'd been practicing, and we both knew where we needed to be, and if we screwed up, what to do. So it was just more fun than anything." At one point in the run, Macdonald actually grabbed his board with his hand and flipped it to Hawk in the middle of a one-handed invert holding onto the top of the wall. Hawk then soared between Macdonald's feet and board. Their performance set a standard for future skateboarders to match.

Bike-riding as an extreme sport has its roots in the 1970s, when the youth of the United States watched the growing sport of motorcycle racing at flat tracks, motocross parks, or on TV. Bike manufacturers were soon selling what they called BMX—Bicycle MotoCross—bikes. They had frames that looked like those of small motorcycles, and the parts were heavier and of higher quality than those of traditional bikes. The use of BMX bikes in the movie *E.T.* created an instant demand for the bikes, which were taken over jumps and across short up and down tracks built especially for them. Some daredevil bike riders started to follow their skateboarding friends into the empty swimming pools and drainage culverts of southern California, and the extreme sport of vertical biking was born.

Dennis McCoy of Kansas City, Missouri, started biking at the age of 13 on a K-Mart special his parents bought him in the 1970s and later switched to BMX bikes as soon as they came out. From 1986 through 1995, he won 10 straight championships.

At 15 Matt "the Condor" Hoffman was expelled from high school because he never showed up. He was always off practicing his tricks on a bike and dusting off the competition in amateur events around the country. So the next year he became a professional bike rider, and at 19 he owned a semitrailer rig with "Hoffman

Dennis McCoy of Kansas City, Missouri, goes completely upside down during the bicycle stunt street competition at the 1996 X Games in Newport, Rhode Island. McCoy crashed while trying to complete this maneuver.

Productions" painted on the side. Too young to drive the rig, he had to hire a driver. He promoted himself at biking events around the country and sold his own brand of bike, the Hoffman Bike, and bike frames. At the same time, Matt was winning gold medals in vert biking at the 1995 and 1996 X Games. In 1997 he placed third.

The only real competition Matt had came from Dave Mirra, winner of 10 X Games medals, including three vert titles in '97, '98, and '99. When the X Games added street bike competition, Dave won the event from 1996 through 1999. In 1998, he combined with Dennis McCoy to win the vert doubles, a crowded and dangerous event with two bikes and two riders on the same ramp at the same time. "Winning gold never gets old," Mirra said. "Winning [the X Games] is the biggest accomplishment right now anybody can have in this sport. I'm on a streak right now, but it can end any time I guess. I'm just going to try to ride my best and come back every year and do the best I can."

A fall with a bike can be dangerous. Almost all vert bikers ride in pain. Most have more pins holding bones together inside their bodies than they have piercing the outside parts. Both Matt Hoffman and Dave Mirra have paid for their fame with more than the sweat of practice. At an event in Texas that was organized by Matt shortly after the 1995 X Games, Dave got his shirt tangled up in the handlebars as he was doing a trick about 10 feet above the platform. He fell hard on top of his machine and tore his spleen in half. Matt went to the hospital with Dave and was quick to

diagnose the injury. He had torn his spleen in a similar accident once and knew the feeling. Riders wear elbow and knee pads as well as full-face motocross helmets to protect themselves against injuries.

Vert bike competitions are judged like other half-pipe sports of boards and skates. A rider is given between a minute and a minute-and a-half to complete a run. Five judges rate each run on difficulty, originality, style, and amplitude—how high above the rim the rider

With the San Francisco-Oakland Transbay bridge in the background, Dave Mirra of Greenville, North Carolina, goes airborne on his bike during a stunt at the 1999 X Games. Mirra is one of the top bicycle stunt riders in the world and has won 10 X Games gold medals.

plays out his twists and somersaults. Soaring high in the air enables the biker to do some tricks that take too long to complete at a lower height: spinning, twists, and contortions; hands on the bars or not, feet on the pedals or not; right side up and head side down. When shown a video of some of his tricks, Dave Mirra said, "It's kind of weird because it always looks a lot harder than it feels." Once the preliminary runs are judged, the top 10 contestants do it again for the medals.

Besides the vert and street competitions, the X Games stages other events for bikes. The dirt bike event resembles the original BMX biking challenges many kids have faced, taking the bike over a dirt jump in an empty lot. In the X Games, riders start on a ramp and must take three jumps over three dirt hills within 20 seconds. Going over each of the jumps is not enough; riders are expected to put a trick or two into each air-time. Each competition requires up to eight runs, providing plenty of opportunities to crash and burn. If a rider tries too much and crashes, he may be eliminated. Yet he must do enough tricks to get the attention of the judges, who will see 30 contestants.

At the 1999 summer X Games in San Francisco, high winds wreaked havoc on the dirt jumping competition, rendering riders unable to perform their usual series of tricks. Gold medal winner T. J. Lavin, who opted to keep his routine simple because of the winds, managed to post the most respectable score. "I never thought you could win the X Games doing just a tail whip, an X-out, 360, and Superman Seat Grab," Lavin told ESPN reporters. "But it happened and I'm really happy I stayed consistent."

At the 1997 X Games, a new bike event was staged: flatland biking. In flatland competition, the rider has between two and three minutes to take his trick bike through a choreographed routine on a flat surface resembling a parking lot. There are no flying tricks, but they must display command of a machine that looks like a cross between a pommel horse in gymnastics and a unicycle with a tail. There are foot pegs at the axles of both wheels to

Matt Hoffman, of Oklahoma City, Oklahoma, began trick riding as a young boy, and soon he was attending competitions around the country. Here, Hoffman practices prior to the men's bike vert finals at the 1997 X Games in San Diego, where he took third place.

stand on. The rider moves back and forth between the front and back wheels or stands on a platform welded just below the seat and throws the bike around himself in contortions and spins.

The bikes themselves are expensive and filled with special parts. The handlebars can spin without tangling the brake lines.

Riders experience little danger in flatland competitions but display great beauty and control. Watching flatland biking is like seeing a cross between the ballet and the circus. Points are deducted if a rider's foot or any other part of his body touches the ground during the run. Points are added for degree of difficulty, style, and working all parts of the bike. Tension builds in the audience as a flawless bike routine comes to a close.

The master of flatlanders in 1997 was Trevor Meyer. Trevor got his start in the living room of his home in Spring Park, Minnesota. With the permission of his very understanding mother, he banged into the walls and scuffed up the floor practicing his moves during the snowbound winter months. Trevor honed his flatland routine to perfection and performed during the halftime of National Basketball Association games for several seasons.

The X Games have more biking events than any other kind of extreme sport in their schedule. Besides BMX and flatland events, the X Games include mountain downhill riding, snow biking, and trials bikes. Mountain and snow biking are speed events. Trials riders, like flatlanders, win their events by being slow and precise. Trials riders take their bikes over boulders, ride along logs, through water and sand, all, ideally, without ever losing their balance and never putting their feet to the ground.

Bikes are the first vehicle that most kids own. A bikc is a kid's first passport to the world outside of the home, a chance to be out exploring on one's own. In short, bikes can be a kid's best friend. They also provide some kids their first chance to invent or participate in an extreme sport.

NEW EXTREME SPORTS

The X Games try to represent to their television audience the competition of the extreme sports just like the Olympic Games represent the competition between the world's best swimmers, for example. But the official games as shown on TV can hardly keep up with the extreme sports explosion of today, as sports with fewer rules, more danger, and more room for individual expression continue to win the hearts of today's youth. In terms of viewing popularity, the X Games are second only to the Olympics among young people today.

With the expansion of the X Games, new disciplines were added, and the number of participants increased. There was also an increase in the number of foreign competitors. Twenty countries were represented at the 1999 X Games, and more than 40 percent of the medals awarded went to international athletes. These numbers were expected to grow, as ESPN expanded its commitment to the X Games in 2000, adding several new qualifying competitions around the globe, including new events in Asia, Europe, and Latin America. ESPN planned to televise these new qualifying events, and the 2000 summer X Games themselves were scheduled to take place August 17–22 in San Francisco, California.

As the X Games grew in popularity, new extreme sports were added. One of these new

Greg Nelson wakeboards during a 1997 competition. Like many of the new extreme sports, wakeboarding first emerged in the 1980s, combining elements of waterskiing and skateboarding.

Kim Csizmazia, from Salt Lake City, Utah, competes in the ice climbing difficulty competition at the 1998 winter X Games in Crested Butte, Colorado. Although the excitement of competition motivates the X Games athletes, they are also inspired by the sense of accomplishment that comes from conquering fear and achieving a victory over oneself.

sports involved jumping over ramps barefoot while being pulled through water at 20 mph.

In 1947, 17-year-old A. G. Hancock stepped out of his boards and became perhaps the first person to water-ski on bare feet. In 1963 the first barefoot national competition was held in Australia. Four years later the Australians were the first to jump barefoot over a water ski ramp. Barefoot jumping eventually became an official extreme sport of the X Games. Not only were jumps a part of it, but spectacular entries into the water (jumping from a hovering heli-copter was an early example) and other tricks performed before a jump were judged as well.

In the 1960s surfboards from the beaches of Hawaii gave rise to skateboards in the 1970s, snowboards in the 1980s, and then to skyboards and sandboards. Attaching a strip of Formica to the bottom of a snowboard produced a surface that slid over tiny sand particles like skis over snow or ice. Desert sand dunes replaced snow-covered mountain sides as locations for X Games events.

One of the newest extreme sports, Ultra-Cross, combines skiers and snowboarders in

Jon Kretchman of Fergus Falls, Minnesota, tries to hang on during the bare-foot jumping finals at the 1996 X Games held in Providence, Rhode Island.

a timed relay race. Developed in 1997, Ultra-Cross competitions were first held at Mt. Rose in the Lake Tahoe region of Nevada in 1998. UltraCross made its X Games debut at the 2000 winter X Games held in Mount Snow, Vermont. This new racing discipline was immediately popular because it provided an opportunity for snowboarders and skiers to compete together in a team effort.

Some new sports, like speed climbing, lend themselves to the traditional ideas of competition—one person or one team trying to best another as in biking, skating, or even barefoot jumping. These are the kinds of sports that are covered by the televised X Games.

But some of these new extreme sports are not competitive. Nor can they be seen by an audience. Some are truly solitary by their very nature. The joys of mountain downhill skiing, sea-kayaking, and mountain biking mostly come from inside the athlete. The satisfaction comes silently from within. For many extreme athletes today, outer silence and inward glow is a purer, better, reward for their courage and tireless practice than a medal or applause.

To confront what lies inside each of us is the final test of an athlete. It is not who else we can best that matters in our lives but whether we can get the best from ourselves. What makes someone somersault into an empty swimming pool on a bicycle? Some of it may be to earn the applause of friends, but certainly most of it must be to confront and subdue the fear and nervousness within.

Professional snowboarder Jim Rippey said, "Every day I get to do something bigger and better than I've ever done. Like taking a trick and going an extra 15 feet bigger. Of course, I'm scared. I don't want to rag-doll and hurt myself—that's where I have to conquer my fear. And kids totally respond to that risk-taking as part of the appeal. When you go out and try something that's a little bit sketchy, you feel great about yourself at the end of the day."

Once someone has conquered the fearful terrors in the pit of the stomach, the feeling of hanging onto a granite mountain side with only your fingertips is a joyous "rush" that tamer sports can't provide. Andy Macdonald, the winner of the skateboarding vertical competition in the 1996 X Games, said, "Fear keeps you in check. Fear protects you." It is achieving this victory over the fear within yourself that makes these sports extreme and gives them their popularity. It is also what makes them valuable. Winning a skateboard competition or climbing a sheer vertical rock face are only memories a moment after they are finished, but the strength of character they take to achieve will last a lifetime.

CHRONOLOGY

1947	A. G. Hancock and Dick Pope Jr. water-ski barefoot (apparently becoming the first to do this).
1959	The first skateboards are sold in stores for $9.95.
1963	Tom Sims invents a snowboard for an eighth grade shop project.
1970s	The term "extreme" is used by French mountain skiers Patrick Vallencourt and Sylvain Saudan to describe their conquest of Chamonix Couloirs. (The term "extreme sports" quickly came to be applied to most new and dangerous sports.)
1973	BMX bikes go on the market.
1976	The first commercial skateboard park opens in Carlsbad, California.
1980	The Olson brothers invent modern in-line roller skates.
1983	ESPN presents a seven-race series for BMX bikes with $45,000 and new cars as prizes.
1984	The first bike stunt contests are held in skateboard parks in California.
1985	The first competition sports climbing event is held in Bardonecchia, Italy.
1987	Joel Cruciani is credited with the first sky surfing free fall.
1989	Snowboarders are allowed to use traditional ski resorts like Squaw Valley, California, and Vail, Colorado.
1990	The first snowboard park opens at Vail Ski Resort.
1993	Street luge is demonstrated before 100,000 fans at Laguna Seca Raceway in California.
1995	The first X Games, held in Newport, Rhode Island, are broadcast on ESPN to a national television audience.
1997	The first winter X Games are held in Big Bear Lake, California.
1999	The first Gravity Games are broadcast on NBC to a national television audience.
2000	Winter X Games break attendance records at Mt. Snow, Vermont.

X GAMES EVENTS

SUMMER 1999

Sky surfing

Sports climbing speed

Sports climbing bouldering

Big air snowboarding

Bicycle stunt street

Bicycle stunt half-pipe

Bicycle stunt flatland

Bicycle dirt jump

Vert triples

Freestyle motocross

Wakeboarding

Street luge dual downhill

Street luge supermass

Skateboarding vert

Skateboarding vert doubles

Skateboarding street

Aggressive in-line street

Aggressive in-line vert

WINTER 2000

Freeskiing

Freeskiing big air

Skiboarding slopestyle

Skiboarding triple air (men)

Snocross

Snow mountain biking

Snowboarding slopestyle

Snowboarder X

Snowboarding big air

Snowboarding superpipe

Ultracross

FURTHER READING

Andrejtschitsch, Jan et al. *Action Skateboarding.* New York: Sterling Publishing, 1992.

Brimner, Larry Dane. *Rolling . . . In Line.* New York: Franklin Watts, 1994.

Carstensen, Karol. *BMX Bikes.* Mankato, Minnesota: Capstone Press, 1991.

Jackson, Jay. *Skateboarding Basics.* Mankato, Minnesota: Capstone Press, 1996.

———— . *Snowboarding Basics.* Mankato, Minnesota: Capstone Press, 1996.

Powell, Mark, and John Svensson. *In-Line Skating.* Champaign, Illinois: Human Kinetics Publishers, 1993.

Youngblut, Shelley, ed. *Way Inside ESPN's X Games.* New York: Hyperion/ESPN Books, 1998.

INDEX

ANN GRAHAM GAINES has been a freelance writer for 15 years. She lives in the woods near Gonzales, Texas, with her family. She especially enjoys writing books that interest her four children.

in the pink

by the same author

the pink adobe cookbook
cooking with a silver spoon

in the pink

rosalea murphy

doubleday

new york   london   toronto   sydney   auckland

published by doubleday

a division of Bantam Doubleday Dell Publishing Group, Inc.
1540 Broadway, New York, New York 10036

doubleday and the portrayal of an anchor
with a dolphin are trademarks of Doubleday,
a division of Bantam Doubleday Dell
Publishing Group, Inc.

Book design by Marysarah Quinn

Library of Congress Cataloging-in-Publication Data
Murphy, Rosalea.
    In the pink / Rosalea Murphy. — 1st ed.
        p.   cm.
    1. Cookery, American—Southwestern style. I. Title.
TX 715.2.S69M86   1993
641.5979—dc20   92-44430
                                                    CIP

1 3 5 7 9 10 8 6 4 2

First Edition

acknowledgments

My *sincere thanks and deep appreciation to:*

Kathy Lynch for her support and understanding and for her special talent in deciphering my handwritten recipes. Thank you, Kathy, for your unfailing good humor and patience through this long culinary journey.

Jamie O'Neill for his expert ability to ensure a perfect match of food and wine.

Meg Ruley who believed in me twice.

My very special thanks to my family and my friends for their support, their comments, and the enthusiastic response of their taste buds while testing and tasting the recipes.

contents

introduction

❦ in the pink

In 1994, The Pink Adobe will celebrate its 50th anniversary. Nineteen forty-four was a grim, exciting, and dangerous time for America and the world. I was trying to function as an independent individual and as an artist. I wanted to paint—to create art—to grow. I was well aware that I could not make a living through my art, even though art makes living worthwhile. So, as an alternative to getting a time-consuming job, what better solution was there than to open a restaurant? I could paint, cook, and support myself, all under one roof. To me, it seemed like a creative inspiration!

I wanted to cater to man's basic need—food. I wanted to start with something very simple and honest—hamburgers, onion soup, apple pie—but to make it the best, presented in the most tempting way possible. And I wanted to create a place with lots of color, texture, and form, and to do it (out of necessity) with the meager materials available: boards, bricks, rope, and paint. And so, in wartime, with sugar, meat, shoes, and fuel rationed, I opened a restaurant. I think I believed that my serving food for other bodies would somehow result in feeding my starving soul and would enable me to pursue my art.

Santa Fe in those days was cherished as a secret pleasure—a cultural center wrapped in old-world charm. The Pink Adobe became the favorite haunt for local artists—John Sloan, Will Shuster, Randall Davey, Oliver LaFarge, and many more. Mark Rothko would visit when he was in town, as well as Mabel Dodge, Freda Lawrence, and

Dorothy Brett. Even Georgia O'Keeffe was an occasional visitor. Harry Partch, the famous composer and maker of exotic instruments, washed dishes at The Pink in exchange for his room and board while completing his well-known score "Highway 66." Richard Diebenkorn came up from Albuquerque to attend our weekend parties.

After hours, we would bring out our red jug wine and something wonderful to eat, listen to Fats Waller and Louis Armstrong records, discuss art and life, and wonder what was going on at Los Alamos, which was referred to as "up on the hill." We were always celebrating something—a birthday, a wedding, the sale of a painting. Each celebration called for a special feast! We had poetry readings, followed by a serving of creative hors d'oeuvres and always the ubiquitous red wine.

Once a month, we had an art show in the dining room, which called for an opening party. Usually several molded mousses surrounded by crackers were placed on tables around the room. Those with seafood were considered quite elegant—a rare delicacy in the desert.

The stumbling block to this early endeavor was that The Pink became so demanding and time-consuming, and I became so absorbed with its survival and unexpected early popularity, that my painting was forced to take a backseat. Several decades passed before I could seriously return to my easel.

Though times change, some things never change at The Pink Adobe. It still occupies the original space, although it has been enlarged by several additions (always in the traditional pueblo style). Its elusive, eclectic decor is still in evidence, although most of the funky furniture is gone, replaced by sturdy tables and chairs that don't wiggle. The walls are still covered with lots of art—some mine and some my friends'. Beautiful murals and handmade pottery made by my daughter, Priscilla, are displayed on the shelves. Louis Armstrong is still singing on tape.

The Pink Adobe remains a focal point for artists. Almost any night in The Dragon Room Bar, one can find a table occupied by local artists—discussing, drinking, and eating. The difference might be in the choice of drinks.

Tequila, vodka, and brandy have replaced the red jug wine. This year we will celebrate our sixth annual self-portrait show. Twenty-five to thirty artists are invited to make images of themselves in a variety of media. It is a very merry event, with judges and prizes, food, and wine. A Celebration of Artists!

The Pink Adobe has strived to maintain its high standards of food preparation throughout the years and has kept its own unique style, while still being aware and taking advantage of all the marvelous ethnic and exotic foods in the markets today. But in its own unorthodox fashion, it has never followed along with the "tres chic" fads and trends that have seen so many restaurants come and go. I have, of course, enjoyed some wonderful innovations in some of those trendy places—though I am not fond of overdoses of cilantro.

To me, food is a pleasure and should be shared. Through this book, I would like to share some of my ideas for entertaining, using easy-to-follow recipes, and to offer suggestions for menus that will help you approach entertaining in your own individual way. Creativity in the kitchen is a true art. Any basic recipe lends itself to subtle variations of flavor and texture that will bring pleasure to the guests—and fame and compliments to the cook.

Keep simplicity in mind and always use the freshest ingredients. *In The Pink* the creative fires still burn as hot as ever.

✒ on entertaining

Dispensing hospitality in a sophisticated yet uncomplicated style is the true purpose of entertaining. It should be the foremost desire of the hostess or host to know that the guests will leave with a lasting and happy memory of the event they have just attended. Every pleasurable experience adds enrichment to our lives, and extending such an experience to others can be a great source of personal fulfillment.

The art of cooking is an important part of the art of living, and entertaining is of the essence of both. The art of cooking can be appreciated by all, from the gastronome with an educated palate to the neophyte gourmet who knows only that a dish might need a little salt.

Creating the setting for whatever event you plan is most important, whether it be grand and formal or more relaxed. I personally prefer simple, casual elegance, but knowing your own style is very important.

Don't be afraid to break away from the conventional. Flower arrangements need not be formal; something from the garden is always cheerful. Make a cornucopia of shining vegetables or fruit, accented with a few flowers. Use your imagination to create conversation-piece still-lifes.

Careful planning is required to create the desired ambiance. Entertaining should be done with confidence and pleasure. Prepare as much as possible ahead of time in order to spend more time with your guests rather than in the kitchen.

Everyone has his or her own gala day to celebrate, an occasion to indulge almost any whim or craving. Though it may seem necessary to have a special occasion to change your eating habits, your menu need not follow the seasons. Fresh fruit and vegetables flown in from faraway places can generally be obtained all year round. Fresh peaches, strawberries, asparagus, exotic lettuces, and more are available even in midwinter.

Most recipes are variations on old themes. It is up to the imaginative and sophisticated cook of today to decide whether to follow a recipe letter for letter or add a personal twist or subtle nuance. Good—sometimes great—recipes are born through experimenting. Updating an old classic can provide fabulous results.

When a departing discerning guest tells you, "There must have been a genius at work in the kitchen!" you'll know that your event has been a success.

Rosalea Murphy
August, 1992

comments on wines

Accompanying Rosalea's delicious, well-tested recipes, you will find suggestions on wines and other beverages that complement the food and the ambiance of Santa Fe's famed Pink Adobe.

Pairing fine wine with great food makes for a truly memorable meal. It is not imperative, however, that you match The Pink Adobe's carefully chosen wines when you prepare these dishes at home. Some wines are not always available in every wine shop, and you may discover other wines you prefer over our selections. Don't be shy about asking for suggestions and stating your price limits when you shop. It's a big world, and there are many good wines just waiting to be discovered and enjoyed.

Vintages change despite the careful vintner's efforts to achieve consistency. One year's product may be more agreeable than another's yield. Many factors determine differences in wines, such as the effects of soil and climate on grapes from different vineyards and different countries. When you find a wine you like, buy a case and store it properly and you will always be prepared to serve exactly what you prefer.

A great meal should stand on its own. Each customer at The Pink Adobe knows we spare no efforts to achieve culinary excellence. That will surely be your objective, too, when you prepare these recipes at home. And the same excellence should be sought in the wine you serve.

We stress the fact that there are no hard-and-fast rules when it comes to individual taste. If you prefer red wine with your meal, so be it. If you like chardonnay with steak, serve it. And if you would rather have beer—it's your choice. The Pink Adobe strives to please its customers, not to dictate what they should eat or drink.

The secret of dining pleasure is very simple. Choose the food you enjoy and the beverage you like to drink. If your favorite wine is not available, ask if a comparable one is.

To those of you who have been our guests, it is our sincere wish that when you prepare Rosalea's recipes at home, you remember your dining experience at The Pink Adobe as a very special occasion. It goes without saying that we hope the wines you serve with your meal are as satisfying as the ones you were served at the restaurant. If you have not yet shared an evening with us at The Pink, we look forward to serving you!

Jamie O'Neill, Wine Steward

brunch and lunch

No meal offers more opportunity for delightful surprise than the combination of a late breakfast and an early lunch—known as brunch. Forget the bacon-and-eggs routine; concentrate on the unusual. With a bit of drama, simple foods artistically presented can be made to seem exotic!

All the menus here are designed to serve 6 unless otherwise noted. Asterisks are used to indicate recipes that are not included in this book.

a santa fe brunch

10

❖

seafood brunch

14

❖

southwestern surprise

18

❖

rio grande brunch

22

❖

dixieland brunch

26

❖

orient express brunch

31

❖

a santa fe brunch

❖

creole marys

fresh fruit bowl*
avocado and green chili mousse
chicken poblano rellenos
jalapeño salsa
flour tortillas*

brown sugar meringue cupcakes

coffee and tea*

❖

*Wonderful with Gruet Blanc de Noirs, méthode
champenoise!*

creole marys

1 ½ ounces Russian
   vodka
4 ounces tomato juice
Dash of Rose's lime juice
Dash of Worcestershire
   sauce
Dash of Tabasco sauce
Celery salt and freshly
   ground pepper, to taste

Mix all ingredients together. Pour over ice in a 12-ounce brandy snifter. Garnish with a combination of the following: celery stick, banana pepper, cherry pepper, jalapeño pepper, lime.

avocado and green chili mousse

Two ¼-ounce envelopes
   unflavored gelatin
¾ cup water
2 cups mashed avocado
½ cup mayonnaise
½ cup sour cream
2 tablespoons lemon juice
1 teaspoon salt
1 tablespoon chopped
   onion
One 4-ounce can chopped
   green chilies
1 small fresh jalapeño
   pepper, chopped fine
Lemon slices, avocado
   slices, and olives, for
   garnish

Sprinkle the gelatin over the water in a small saucepan. Stir over low heat until dissolved. Set aside.

In a large bowl, mix the avocado with all remaining ingredients. Stir in the dissolved gelatin and pour into a greased 6-cup ring mold. Chill until firm. Unmold mousse onto a serving platter.

Garnish with lemon, avocado slices, and olives.

chicken poblano rellenos

7 medium to large
poblano chilies

Roast the chilies under medium flame in preheated broiler until they blister on all sides. Wrap in plastic wrap and allow them to sweat for 5 minutes. When cool, peel the chilies, slit one side, and seed. Set aside 6 of the chilies.

❧ chili sauce:

1 cup hot water
½ cup chopped onion
1 medium tomato,
    chopped
1 clove garlic, chopped
1 cup chicken stock
¼ cup olive oil

Soak the remaining chili in the hot water for 15 minutes; drain and puree in a blender along with the onion, tomato, garlic, and chicken stock. Heat the oil in a sauté pan and cook the puree over low heat, stirring constantly, for about 3 minutes. Reserve.

❧ chicken filling:

1 pound cooked chicken
meat, ground
¾ cup reserved Chili
    Sauce
¼ cup raisins, soaked in
    water and drained
¼ cup sliced almonds
Salt and pepper, to taste
8 eggs, separated
½ cup flour
2 ½ to 3 cups peanut oil,
    for frying

In a small bowl, beat the egg yolks. In a separate bowl, beat the egg whites until stiff. Fold the two together. Set aside. Combine the chicken, chili sauce, raisins, almonds, salt and pepper and gently stir to mix well. Fill each reserved roasted chili pepper with Chicken Filling.

Secure each pepper with toothpicks to retain the shape and to keep the stuffing from falling out. Dust each pepper lightly with flour, dip into reserved egg mixture, and fry in hot peanut oil until brown.

Serve with bottled salsa, or make your own (recipe follows).

jalapeño salsa

makes about 2 cups

2 cups peeled tomatoes
1 small onion, chopped
2 green onions, chopped
5 small fresh jalapeño
    peppers, stemmed and
    cut in pieces
1 small zucchini, diced
1 clove garlic
½ teaspoon chopped fresh
    cilantro
Salt, to taste

Put all ingredients in a blender. Process until coarsely chopped; 10 to 12 seconds only! Do not pulverize! Salsa should have a crunchy texture.

brown sugar meringue cupcakes

1 ¾ cups cake flour
2 teaspoons baking
    powder
½ teaspoon salt
1 cup sugar
⅓ cup vegetable
    shortening (Crisco)
1 egg, separated
½ cup milk
1 teaspoon vanilla extract

↗ topping:

1 egg white (from
    separated egg)
2 tablespoons sweet cocoa
½ cup brown sugar
¼ cup pecans, chopped

Preheat oven to 350°. Sift together the flour, baking powder, and salt. Cream the sugar and shortening until creamy. Add the egg yolk and beat thoroughly. Add flour mixture and milk alternately. Beat until smooth after each addition. Stir in vanilla.

Grease 12 muffin tins. Fill cups halfway with batter.

To prepare the topping, beat the egg white until stiff and gradually fold in the cocoa and brown sugar. Pile lightly on the cupcakes. Sprinkle with pecans.

Bake for 30 minutes.

seafood brunch

❖

rosalitas

melon slices with fresh strawberries*
baked fish fillets in cheese sauce
herbed rice
cucumber salad with cucumber dressing
southwest corn bread

pink adobe chocolate mousse

coffee and tea*

❖

Try 1991 Flora Springs Sauvignon Blanc with this seafood brunch.

rosalitas

1 ounce gold tequila
¾ ounce Triple Sec
1 ½ ounces cranberry juice
½ ounce freshly squeezed lime juice
¼ ounce Grand Marnier
1 slice lime

(from *the pink adobe cookbook*)

makes 1 serving

Pour all ingredients, except Grand Marnier and lime slice, over ice and shake. Splash with Grand Marnier and strain into a 7-ounce stemmed wine glass. Squeeze lime slice on top.

baked fish fillets in cheese sauce

2 pounds fish fillets (sole, flounder, haddock, halibut, tuna, or cod)
Tabasco sauce, to taste
Salt and pepper, to taste

Preheat oven to 375°. Pat fish dry. Place in a 10-inch baking pan. Sprinkle with Tabasco, salt and pepper, and set aside. Prepare the Cheese Sauce.

❧ cheese sauce:

2 tablespoons butter
2 tablespoons flour
1 ½ cups half-and-half or milk
¾ cup shredded Gruyère cheese
Pinch each: salt and cayenne
½ teaspoon dry mustard

Melt the butter in a saucepan over medium heat. Stir and blend in the flour. Slowly stir in the half-and-half. When the sauce is smooth and has thickened, stir in the cheese. Season with salt, cayenne, and mustard. Stir until the cheese has melted.

❧ garnish:

Chopped parsley
Paprika

Pour Cheese Sauce over the fish, and bake for 10 to 15 minutes. Garnish with chopped parsley and paprika.

herbed rice

2 tablespoons butter
¼ cup chopped green
  onions
¼ cup chopped green
  chilies
¼ teaspoon salt
Pinch each: thyme,
  rosemary, parsley
1 ½ cups long grain rice
1 ½ cups water

Melt the butter in a 2-quart saucepan. Lightly sauté the onions and green chilies. Add seasonings. Stir in the rice and water. Bring to a boil, lower heat, and cook for about 25 minutes, until all the water is absorbed.

cucumber salad with cucumber dressing

❧ salad:

4 medium cucumbers,
  peeled and sliced paper
  thin
1 small onion, peeled and
  sliced paper thin
¼ teaspoon salt
¼ teaspoon pepper
⅛ teaspoon fresh or dried
  dill weed
⅛ teaspoon sugar

❧ cucumber
dressing:

½ cup grated cucumber
½ cup balsamic or cider
  vinegar
1 teaspoon salt
½ teaspoon pepper
¼ teaspoon sugar
1 ½ cups olive oil

Combine all salad ingredients in a large bowl. Set aside.

To prepare the Cucumber Dressing, place all ingredients except the olive oil in a screw-top jar. Shake to blend well. Add the olive oil and shake to blend. Pour over salad, only as much as is needed to moisten cucumbers and onion.

Let the salad marinate in the refrigerator until thoroughly chilled (1 hour or more).

southwest corn bread

makes 12 muffins,
or can be baked in a 10-inch iron skillet

1 cup flour
1 tablespoon baking
    powder
1 teaspoon sugar
¾ teaspoon salt
1 ½ cups yellow cornmeal
¼ cup chopped fresh
    jalapeño pepper
1 egg
1 cup milk
6 tablespoons butter,
    melted

Preheat oven to 375°. Mix together the dry ingredients and jalapeño. Stir in the egg and milk. Fold the butter into the mixture. Oil muffin tins or a 10-inch iron skillet. (If using skillet, heat after oiling.) Spoon in batter and bake for 20 to 25 minutes.

pink adobe chocolate mousse

4 squares (4 ounces)
    semisweet chocolate
½ package (2 ounces)
    German's sweet
    chocolate
1 tablespoon strong black
    coffee
1 teaspoon instant
    espresso granules
¾ cup sugar
¼ cup water
4 eggs, separated
1 tablespoon butter
1 teaspoon rum or ½
    teaspoon rum extract
1 cup heavy cream,
    whipped firm
Grated orange peel, for
    garnish
Grated semisweet
    chocolate, for garnish

Combine the chocolates, coffee, and espresso and melt in the top of a double boiler. In a saucepan, boil the sugar and water until syrupy. In a bowl, beat the egg yolks. Stir the sugar syrup and egg yolks into the melted chocolate; mix well and remove from heat. Immediately add the butter and rum.

Place the pan in a bowl of ice to cool. Beat the egg whites until stiff. With a rubber spatula, fold egg whites into the cooled chocolate and then fold in the whipped cream. Reserve a little cream for garnish.

Turn the mousse into a lightly oiled 1½-quart mold, or 6 to 8 individual serving glasses. Chill for several hours. Unmold mousse onto a plate, or serve in glasses. Garnish with reserved whipped cream, grated orange peel, and/or grated chocolate.

southwestern surprise

❖

margarita gold

cruditiés*
corn bread upside-down cake with
ham and green chili sauce
gazpacho salad

praline pie

coffee and tea*

❖

1990 Pine Ridge Chenin Blanc is a good wine choice.

margarita gold

(from *the pink adobe cookbook*)

makes 1 serving

1 ounce gold tequila
(preferably Herradura)
¾ ounce Triple Sec or
Grand Marnier
1 ½ ounces bottled sweet-
and-sour mix❖
½ ounce freshly squeezed
lime juice
Salt
1 lime, cut into wedges

Combine the tequila, Triple Sec, sweet-and-sour mix, and lime juice. Shake with ice.

Rub rim of a large-bowled stemmed glass, such as a 12-ounce snifter, with cut lime. Dip the rim of the glass in a bowl of salt. Strain contents of the shaker into the glass.

Garnish with a lime wedge.

variation: For frozen Margarita Golds, mix ingredients in a blender with ice.

❖ Bottled sweet-and-sour mix is available in supermarkets and wherever liquor is sold.

corn bread upside-down cake with ham and green chili sauce

4 tablespoons butter
½ cup flour
1 ½ teaspoons baking
  powder
1 tablespoon granulated
  sugar
¾ teaspoon salt
1 ½ cups yellow cornmeal
1 egg
¾ cup milk
3 tablespoons butter,
  melted
½ cup brown sugar
One 15-ounce can sliced
  pineapple (8 slices)
5 slices baked ham, ¼
  inch thick
Grapes or cherries, for
  garnish

Grease a deep 10-inch ovenproof skillet with the 4 table-spoons butter. Heat in a 200° oven while assembling other ingredients.

Sift together the flour, baking powder, granulated sugar, and salt. Add the cornmeal and mix well. In a separate bowl, beat the egg, then add the milk and 3 tablespoons melted butter and stir together. Pour the egg mixture into the dry ingredients. Combine, using a few strokes.

Remove the skillet from the oven. Sprinkle the brown sugar into the skillet and arrange the pineapple slices over it in one layer. Place the ham slices over the pineapple and pour cornmeal batter over all.

Turn oven temperature to 350° and bake for 25 to 30 minutes. Meanwhile, prepare the sauce (recipe follows).

When corn bread is baked, turn it out, upside down, on a platter. Garnish with grapes or cherries and serve with Green Chili Sauce.

❧ green chili sauce:

2 tablespoons butter
2 fresh green chilies,❖ 3
  inches long, chopped
2 tablespoons flour
1 cup chicken broth
1 cup half-and-half
Salt, to taste

Melt the butter in a 1-quart saucepan. Sauté the chopped chilies for ½ minute. Add the flour and mix. Slowly pour in the chicken broth; stir until sauce thickens. Gradually blend in the cream. Add salt to taste.

❖ If fresh chilies are not available, substitute one 4-ounce can of chopped green chilies.

note: For a speedy breakfast, substitute one 13-ounce box yellow corn bread mix for the homemade corn bread.

gazpacho salad

1 medium red onion
1 large cucumber
1 green bell pepper
1 yellow bell pepper
6 large tomatoes
½ cup dry French-bread
   crumbs

❧ dressing:

6 tablespoons olive oil
2 tablespoons balsamic
   vinegar
1 small clove garlic,
   crushed
Salt and pepper, to taste
Pinch of mustard

Peel and slice the onion very thin. Slice the unpeeled cucumber very thin. Seed and core the peppers; cut into thin strips. Peel and slice the tomatoes very thin.

In a large glass salad bowl, arrange alternating layers of vegetables and lightly sprinkled bread crumbs—a layer of onions, a layer of crumbs, a layer of cucumber, a layer of crumbs, and so on.

Place all dressing ingredients in a screw-top jar and shake to blend. Pour over the salad and chill thoroughly.

praline pie

4 eggs
½ cup sugar
3 tablespoons flour
Pinch of salt
1 cup dark Karo syrup
1 cup pecans, chopped
1 teaspoon vanilla extract
One 9-inch unbaked pie
   shell
½ cup pecan halves
Heavy cream, whipped
   (optional)

Preheat oven to 325°.

Beat the eggs lightly. Add the sugar, flour, salt, syrup, chopped pecans, and vanilla. Stir until blended. Pour into the pie shell. Arrange the pecan halves on top.

Bake for 50 minutes. Serve with whipped cream, if desired.

rio grande brunch

❖

tequila sunrise cocktail

marinated melon balls
sausage and oysters in puff pastry shells
creamed spinach

mexican custard

coffee and tea*

❖

*Try 1990 Alexander Valley Vineyards Riesling for your wine
selection, and serve spritzers with a splash of Campari (optional)
and a twist of lemon.*

tequila sunrise cocktail

makes 1 serving

Crushed ice
2 ounces tequila
  (Herradura or Sauza)
Orange juice
1 tablespoon Grenadine

Fill a 12-ounce glass with crushed ice. Add tequila. Fill glass with orange juice. Pour Grenadine over top.

marinated melon balls

2 small cantaloupe
1 small honeydew melon
4 or 5 teaspoons freshly
  squeezed lime juice
½ cup honey, warmed

Cut the melons in half. Remove seeds. With a melon ball cutter, scoop melon balls from all three melons and reserve the shells. In a large bowl, combine melon balls with the lime juice and honey. Return to reserved shells.

Decorate with edible flowers, if available.

sausage and oysters in puff pastry shells

6 frozen puff pastry shells
½ pound frozen breakfast
  sausage links
1 pint fresh shucked
  oysters, drained, and
  liquid reserved
2 tablespoons butter
½ cup sliced fresh
  mushrooms
½ cup green onions,
  thinly sliced
2 tablespoons flour
1 cup beef broth, plus ½
  cup reserved oyster
  liquid
¼ cup dry sherry
½ cup heavy cream
¼ teaspoon nutmeg
¼ teaspoon salt (optional)
½ teaspoon Tabasco
  sauce
Chopped parsley, for
  garnish

Bake the pastry shells according to directions on package. Cut the sausage in ¼-inch-thick circles and brown. Set aside. Chop the oysters coarsely and set aside with the sausage.

Heat the butter in a heavy saucepan. Sauté the mushrooms and onions in the butter for a few minutes. Stir in the flour. Slowly add the beef broth and oyster liquid, stirring. Stir in the sherry. Continue to stir a few minutes, until thickened, then stir in cream and seasonings. Add oysters and sausage, stir, and heat for 5 minutes. Fill the pastry shells and garnish with chopped parsley.

creamed spinach

thick white sauce:

2 tablespoons butter
2 tablespoons flour
¾ cup half-and-half
¼ teaspoon salt
¼ teaspoon Tabasco
  sauce

1 ½ tablespoons butter
¼ cup finely chopped
  green onions
Two 10-ounce packages
  frozen chopped
  spinach, thawed
Salt, pepper, and nutmeg,
  to taste

To make the white sauce, melt the butter in a heavy saucepan. Stir in the flour and mix thoroughly. Slowly add the half-and-half, stirring constantly until sauce is smooth and thickened. Stir in the salt and Tabasco.

Melt the butter in a heavy skillet. Add the green onions and sauté for 2 or 3 minutes. Add the spinach and sauté until spinach is hot—about 2 minutes. Season with salt, pepper, and a dash of nutmeg. Stir in the hot Thick White Sauce. Serve immediately.

mexican custard

❧ caramel coating:

½ cup sugar
½ cup water

❧ custard:

2 cups milk
3 eggs
2 egg yolks
½ cup sugar
¼ teaspoon nutmeg
1 teaspoon vanilla extract
Garnish: nutmeg

Lightly grease 6 custard cups.

In a heavy saucepan, boil ½ cup sugar and the water until sugar caramelizes and turns brown. Pour a tablespoon of the syrup in each custard cup and swirl around to coat the cup. Preheat oven to 350°.

To prepare the custard, heat the milk in a saucepan until hot but not boiling. In the top of a double boiler, combine the eggs, egg yolks, ½ cup sugar, nutmeg, and vanilla. Slowly add the hot milk. Stir well to mix.

Divide mixture among the caramel-coated custard cups. Place cups in a deep baking pan or a deep-dish pizza pan. Add water to pan to come ¾ of the way up sides of custard cups. Bake custard 45 to 55 minutes. Test with a knife inserted in center. If knife comes out clean, the custards are done. When cool, invert onto individual plates and sprinkle lightly with nutmeg.

dixieland brunch

❖

bloody marys elaborate

green chili-cheese dip
chicken hash in grits ring
pickled peaches
hot biscuits
or
hot buttermilk biscuits

frozen kahlúa-mocha mousse

coffee and tea*

❖

For this Dixieland Brunch, serve Dixie beer, such as Blackened Voodoo; 1979 Robert Mondavi Sauvignon Blanc Botrytis; and coffee with chickory.

bloody marys elaborate

1 quart tomato juice
½ cup freshly squeezed
   lemon juice
2 tablespoons white
   horseradish
Pepper, to taste
2 dashes Rose's lime juice
2 dashes Worcestershire
   sauce
2 dashes Tabasco sauce
1 ½ cups Russian vodka

Mix all ingredients in a large pitcher. Pour over ice in 12-ounce brandy glasses. Garnish with any or all of the following: celery stick, scallion, pickled okra, banana pepper, cherry pepper, jalapeño pepper, lime slice.

variation: Substitute tequila for vodka and canned clamato juice for tomato juice. Garnish with a fresh boiled shrimp.

green chili - cheese dip

One 8-ounce package
   cream cheese, softened
1 cup sour cream
1 cup diced green chilies
½ teaspoon finely
   chopped fresh jalapeño
   pepper
½ cup finely chopped
   green onions
Half-and-half for
   thinning, if necessary
1 tablespoon piñon nuts,
   chopped fine

Combine all ingredients except the piñon nuts and process in an electric blender. Stir in the piñon nuts. Cover and refrigerate dip for several hours to blend flavors. Serve with corn chips.

chicken hash in grits ring

Molded rings can lend an elegant, festive touch to an informal and casual gathering. They are relatively simple to make and well worth the compliments they inspire. I give you recipes for two rings: one of grits and one of rice (See Orient Express Brunch). This grits ring takes more than an hour to cook, so plan accordingly.

❧ grits ring:

4 cups water
1 teaspoon salt
1 cup quick-cooking grits
3 tablespoons butter
3 eggs, separated
¾ cup shredded Cheddar cheese

Preheat oven to 350°. Bring the water and salt to a boil. Stir in the grits and cook until thickened. (Quick-cooking grits take about 5 minutes.) Remove from heat. Add the butter, cover, and let stand until cool.

In a small bowl, beat the egg yolks. In another bowl, beat the egg whites until very stiff. Stir the egg yolks and cheese into the grits mixture. Fold in the beaten egg whites.

Generously grease a 10-inch ring mold. Put the grits into the mold and place the mold in a baking pan containing 1 inch of water. Bake for 1 hour (cooking time may vary, depending on your oven), until the top is golden brown. Cool for 10 to 15 minutes before removing from mold.

To unmold Grits Ring, run a silver knife around the sides of the mold to loosen. Invert onto a large platter.

❧ chicken hash:

½ cup (1 stick) butter
¼ cup chopped onion
½ cup chopped celery
3 tablespoons flour
1 ½ cups warm chicken broth
2 tablespoons heavy cream
2 tablespoons Madeira wine
1 teaspoon salt
¼ teaspoon pepper
¼ teaspoon cayenne
3 cups cooked and diced chicken
1 ½ cups peeled and diced cooked potatoes

Melt the butter in a heavy saucepan. Lightly sauté the onion and celery for a few minutes. Stir in the flour and cook over medium heat for 2 minutes. Slowly pour in the chicken broth and stir until thickened. Stir in the cream and Madeira.

If sauce is too thick, add a little more cream. Add seasonings and gently stir in chicken and potatoes. Heat through. Pour the Chicken Hash into center of the unmolded Grits Ring. Serve immediately.

pickled peaches

One 16-ounce can peach
halves, in heavy syrup,
drained, syrup reserved
¼ cup honey
¼ cup orange juice
½ cup white vinegar
½ teaspoon whole cloves

In a large saucepan, combine the peach syrup, honey, orange juice, vinegar, and cloves. Bring mixture to a boil and simmer for 5 minutes. Add the drained peaches. Simmer 2 or 3 minutes more. Remove from heat.

Pour peaches and liquid into a glass bowl and cover. Refrigerate overnight before serving.

hot biscuits

2 cups flour
4 teaspoons baking
powder
1 teaspoon salt
1 tablespoon lard or
vegetable shortening
⅔ cup milk
3 tablespoons milk or
cream, for brushing
tops

For a standard, foolproof biscuit, try this.

Preheat oven to 450°. Sift the flour with the baking powder and salt. Crumble in the shortening to make a coarse mixture. Gradually add the ⅔ cup milk. Mix until dough is soft, turn out onto a floured surface, and with floured hands, pat dough out to ½-inch thickness and cut into rounds.

Place biscuits 1 inch apart on an oiled baking sheet. Brush with milk. Bake until biscuits are puffed and brown, about 12 minutes.

hot buttermilk biscuits

2 cups flour
2 teaspoons baking
powder
1 teaspoon baking soda
¼ teaspoon salt
¼ cup vegetable
shortening
1 cup buttermilk
3 tablespoons milk or
cream, for brushing top

Follow instructions for Hot Biscuits.

frozen kahlúa - mocha mousse

1 ½ cups heavy cream
2 tablespoons instant
  espresso coffee granules
¼ cup sugar
½ cup semisweet
  chocolate chips
2 eggs, plus 2 egg yolks
½ teaspoon vanilla extract
2 tablespoons Kahlúa
1 tablespoon grated
  orange peel, for garnish
½ cup chopped pecans,
  for garnish

Measure ¼ cup of the cream into a small saucepan. Mix in the espresso coffee and sugar and slowly heat until coffee and sugar are dissolved. Set aside. Melt the chocolate in the top of a double boiler or in the microwave (about 2 minutes). In an electric blender, blend the eggs and egg yolks for 2 minutes. Add the coffee mixture, vanilla, and remaining cream. Blend at medium speed for ½ minute. Add the melted chocolate and Kahlúa. Blend until smooth.

Divide mousse equally among six ½-cup ramekins. Freeze for several hours until set. Sprinkle with grated orange peel and chopped nuts. Let sit for 5 or 6 minutes at room temperature before serving.

note: Make this the night before, or allow sufficient time for freezing.

variation: Use Grand Marnier instead of Kahlúa.

orient express brunch

❖

margaritas*

shrimp pâté
curried turkey in rice ring
condiments (chopped peanuts, bacon, coconut,
chutney, banana flakes)*
snow peas with water chestnuts
banana corn muffins

chocolate covered strawberries

coffee and tea*

❖

1987 Jordan "J" is a fine choice.

shrimp pâté

One 3-ounce package
  cream cheese, softened
2 tablespoons lemon juice
½ teaspoon prepared
  white horseradish
1 small green onion,
  chopped
3 tablespoons mayonnaise
1 hard-cooked egg
½ teaspoon salt
½ teaspoon chopped fresh
  jalapeño pepper
1 pound cooked shrimp,
  finely chopped

Place all ingredients except shrimp in a blender and process until smooth. Add the shrimp and mix with a rubber spatula to distribute evenly.

Transfer pâté to a decorative bowl or crock and serve with assorted crackers.

curried turkey in rice ring

❦ rice ring:

1 teaspoon chopped green
  onion
1 teaspoon chopped celery
1 teaspoon chopped green
  bell pepper
1 teaspoon chopped
  parsley
3 cups cooked rice
¼ cup (½ stick) butter,
  melted

Preheat oven to 350°. Mix the onion, celery, bell pepper, and parsley with the rice. Press firmly into a well-greased 10-inch ring mold. Pour melted butter over top. Set the mold in a pan containing 1 inch of water and bake for 20 to 25 minutes.

Let mold stand for 5 minutes. Loosen edges with a silver knife and unmold Rice Ring onto a serving platter. Fill center with Curried Turkey (recipe follows).

⫷ curried turkey:

½ cup (1 stick) butter
4 tart apples, peeled,
    cored, and chopped, or
    one 16-ounce can pie
    apples, chopped (not
    pie filling)
2 medium onions, peeled
    and finely chopped
¼ cup seedless raisins
¼ cup lemon juice
¼ cup curry powder
1 tablespoon cayenne
¼ teaspoon ground ginger
⅛ teaspoon thyme
1 teaspoon salt
2 tablespoons flour
1 ½ cups chicken broth
1 cup heavy cream
3 cups cooked and diced
    turkey

Melt the butter in a 2-quart saucepan. Sauté, but do not brown, the apples and onions for 5 minutes. Add the raisins, lemon juice, curry powder, cayenne, ginger, thyme, and salt. Mix well. Stir in the flour. Add the chicken broth, followed by the cream. Stir and cook until thickened. Mix in the turkey. If the mixture is too thick, add a little more cream.

Pour Curried Turkey into the center of the Rice Ring. Serve immediately, accompanied by a selection of condiments (see page 31) in small bowls.

3 tablespoons oil
    (preferably sesame oil)
1 tablespoon finely
    chopped fresh
    gingerroot
One 8-ounce can sliced
    water chestnuts,
    drained
1 pound snow peas, or
    two 8-ounce packages
    frozen snow peas,
    thawed, trimmed
    diagonally at each end
½ teaspoon sugar
½ teaspoon salt
2 tablespoons sherry

snow peas with water chestnuts

Heat the oil, add the gingerroot, and stir-fry for 30 seconds. Add the water chestnuts and stir-fry for 2 minutes. Add the snow peas and stir-fry for 3 minutes. Season with sugar and salt. Toss with sherry.

Serve immediately.

banana corn muffins

1 cup flour
¼ cup sugar
¾ cup yellow cornmeal
1 tablespoon baking
   powder
½ teaspoon salt
1 cup mashed ripe
   banana
½ cup milk
⅓ cup vegetable oil
1 egg
½ cup pecan pieces

Preheat oven to 400°. Sift the flour with the sugar, corn-meal, baking powder, and salt. Beat the banana with the milk, oil, and egg. Combine the flour mixture with the banana mixture. Add the pecans. Stir until moistened. Fill 6 well-greased muffin cups ⅔ full. Bake 15 to 18 minutes. Test muffins for doneness. Cool 10 minutes before removing from tin.

variation: Use 1 cup chopped apples in place of the banana.

chocolate covered strawberries

1 pound semisweet
   chocolate bits
12 large strawberries with
   stems

Melt the chocolate in the top of a double boiler, stirring constantly until smooth. Hold strawberries by their stems and dip each one halfway into the melted chocolate. Cool on a sheet of waxed paper.

picnics

Everyone loves a picnic, whether the gathering be for two or for a crowd. Dining outdoors can be an exhilarating experience—under a tree, by a stream, or just in your own backyard.

There are picnics for all seasons and for all occasions. So match your mood to the seasons and pack a feast to enjoy in the great outdoors. It may be just a sandwich, fruit, and a bottle of wine, or something quite elaborate. Whatever you choose, make your picnic a special occasion.

All the menus here are designed to serve 6 unless otherwise noted. Asterisks are used to indicate recipes that are not included in this book.

aspen - viewing picnic

In northern New Mexico in early October, the aspens in the mountains begin to turn an incredible golden color. Beneath the clear, intense blue sky, they are an unbelievable sight.

❖

pear and apple spread with ginger cream cheese
turkey loaf
cranberry chutney
croissants*
three bean salad
bundt coffee cake
cookies*
mocha in a thermos*

❖

For your wine selection, try a 1990 Duckhorn Sauvignon Blanc, Napa Valley, or a 1987 Sterling Vineyards Pinot Noir, Winery Lake.

pear and apple spread with ginger cream cheese

1 ripe pear
1 ripe Delicious or Golden Delicious apple
Freshly squeezed lemon juice

Core the pear and apple and cut into 6 slices each. Sprinkle with lemon juice.

Combine ginger and cream cheese in a small bowl.

Place the fruit slices on a plate to take to the picnic. Cover tightly with plastic wrap. Can be refrigerated several hours if desired. When ready to eat, spread the fruit slices with the gingered cream cheese.

❧ ginger cream cheese:

One 8-ounce package cream cheese, softened
4 tablespoons finely diced candied ginger

turkey loaf

2 pounds ground raw turkey
1 ½ cups soft bread crumbs
½ cup chopped celery
½ cup chopped onion
¼ cup chopped green bell pepper
½ cup chopped tomato
1 small, fresh jalapeño pepper, finely chopped
1 tablespoon piñon nuts
Pinch each: marjoram, rosemary, salt
1 egg, beaten
4 tablespoons ketchup
¼ cup evaporated milk, or enough to hold loaf together
Sprinkle of chopped parsley

Preheat oven to 350°. In a large bowl, combine the turkey with the bread crumbs, celery, onion, green pepper, tomato, jalapeño, piñon nuts, and seasonings. Add the egg and 2 tablespoons of the ketchup. Mix well. Slowly mix in the milk.

Transfer the mixture to a 9 × 5 × 3-inch greased loaf pan. Spread the remaining 2 tablespoons ketchup over the top of the loaf and sprinkle with parsley.

Bake for 50 to 55 minutes, or until the top is lightly browned. When cool, remove loaf from the pan and wrap in foil. Don't forget to take along a sharp knife!

cranberry chutney

2 cups raw cranberries
1 lemon, unpeeled, seeded
   and chopped
1 clove garlic, minced
1 small onion, chopped
1 cup golden raisins
1 ¼ cups brown sugar
1 fresh jalapeño pepper,
   chopped
½ teaspoon red pepper
   flakes
1 teaspoon salt
2 ounces preserved ginger,
   coarsely chopped
1 cup cider vinegar

Combine all ingredients in a large saucepan. Simmer until thick, about 1 to 1½ hours. Stir frequently.

Put the cooled chutney in a plastic container to take to the picnic.

Make croissant sandwiches using a slice of turkey loaf with a tablespoon or more of Cranberry Chutney and green or red leaf lettuce.

croissants:

Split and spread lightly with mayonnaise. Pack croissants in a pastry box. Cover with foil. Put lettuce leaves in a plastic bag. Place all in a cooler.

n o t e : An excellent "fast food" version of the croissant sandwich is to spread the croissant with soft spiced cheese (herbed, aloutte, garlic) and use smoked turkey slices from the deli, leaf lettuce, and tomato preserves (Knott's Berry Farm or Crosse & Blackwell are good brands).

three bean salad

One 8-ounce can
  garbanzo beans
One 8-ounce can green
  beans
One 15-ounce can black
  beans
½ cup chopped green
  onions
½ cup chopped celery
One 8-ounce can chopped
  ripe olives
Green Peppercorn
  Dressing (recipe
  follows)

Drain the beans in a colander. Mix with the remaining ingredients. Toss with Green Peppercorn Dressing. Chill for several hours. Pack in plastic containers.

green peppercorn dressing:

¼ cup balsamic vinegar
2 drops garlic juice (use a
  garlic press or bottled
  garlic juice)
1 teaspoon salt
¼ teaspoon sugar
1 teaspoon green
  peppercorns
1 cup olive oil

Place all ingredients except the olive oil in a screw-top jar. Shake to blend. Add oil and shake again. Shake well before using.

bundt coffee cake

⅓ cup brown sugar
⅓ cup chopped walnuts
½ teaspoon cinnamon
1 cup granulated sugar
½ cup (1 stick) butter,
    softened
2 eggs
1 tablespoon strong coffee
1 teaspoon vanilla extract
1 ¾ cups flour
2 teaspoons baking
    powder
1 teaspoon baking soda
½ teaspoon salt
1 cup sour cream

Preheat oven to 350°. Combine the brown sugar with the walnuts and cinnamon. Set aside.

In large bowl, beat the granulated sugar and butter together until well blended. Beat in the eggs, one at a time, until well blended. Stir in the coffee and vanilla.

In a separate bowl, mix together the flour, baking powder, soda, and salt. Add the flour mixture to the butter mixture, alternating with the sour cream. Beat until well blended.

Pour half the batter into a greased bundt pan. Cover with half the walnut mixture. Pour the remaining batter over the walnuts and spread with remaining walnut mixture on top.

Bake for about 1 hour. Test for doneness after 50 minutes. Cool partially before removing from pan.

Top with Coffee Glaze while cake is still warm. Dust with confectioners sugar before serving.

❧ coffee glaze:

1 cup confectioners sugar
2 tablespoons instant
    espresso coffee granules
1 tablespoon hot water
½ teaspoon heavy cream
¼ teaspoon vanilla extract

Combine all ingredients and beat until smooth. Pour over the warm cake.

classic picnic

❖

fried buttermilk chicken
to please a poet potato salad
microwave pickles

layered cream cheese brownies

❖

*Serve with Sierra Nevada Pale Ale and 1989 Parker
Johannisberg Riesling, Santa Barbara.*

fried buttermilk chicken

6 chicken drumsticks
6 chicken thighs
3 chicken breasts, cut in half
1 tablespoon or more of coarse ground black pepper
2 cups buttermilk
1 ½ to 3 cups peanut oil, for frying
1 ½ cups flour
1 teaspoon salt

Generously sprinkle each piece of chicken with pepper. Place peppered chicken in a large glass or stainless-steel bowl, cover tightly and toss with the buttermilk. Marinate in the refrigerator at least 2 hours, or overnight.

Preheat the oil in a deep fryer to 375°, or use a large skillet. Combine the flour and salt in a large paper bag. Shake chicken pieces, a few at a time, in the bag with the flour. Place a few pieces of chicken in the hot oil. Reduce heat to 350° for the deep fryer; to medium heat for a skillet. Cover and fry for 15 minutes, turning to brown all sides, until chicken is nicely browned. Drain on paper towels.

Repeat process until all chicken is done.

Take the chicken to the picnic in a box. Put waxed paper between the layers.

to please a poet potato salad

1 to 1 ½ pounds unpeeled new potatoes (6 to 8 potatoes)
1 small green onion, finely chopped
½ teaspoon salt
½ teaspoon freshly ground pepper
Anchovy and Mustard Dressing (recipe follows)

makes 4 to 6 servings

Boil potatoes in water to cover until easily pierced by a fork (15 to 20 minutes). While potatoes are cooking, prepare the dressing.

When the potatoes are cool enough to handle, peel and slice thin. Toss with the green onion, salt, and pepper. With a rubber spatula, gently combine the dressing with the potatoes until nicely coated.

Place in a portable serving dish.

1/3 cup olive oil
3 tablespoons mild cider
    vinegar
2 teaspoons prepared
    mustard
1 teaspoon anchovy paste

❧ anchovy and mustard dressing:

Place all ingredients in a food processor and, with on-and-off movement, process until thoroughly blended.

microwave pickles

makes about 2 quarts

2 cups water
1 cup sugar
1 cup white vinegar
2 teaspoons pickling spice
1 teaspoon salt
1 teaspoon dry mustard
1 teaspoon turmeric
6 medium cucumbers,
    peeled and thinly sliced
2 medium onions, peeled
    and thinly sliced

In a 2-quart glass bowl, combine the water, sugar, vinegar, pickling spice, salt, mustard, and turmeric. Microwave on high until mixture boils, about 5 to 7 minutes.

Stir in the cucumbers and onions. Continue cooking on high until mixture comes to a rolling boil, about 8 minutes. Remove from the microwave and let cool.

Cover and refrigerate until pickles are well chilled; overnight is advised. Transport to the picnic in plastic covered containers.

Will keep in the refrigerator for about 10 days.

layered cream cheese brownies

¾ cup semisweet chocolate chips
3 tablespoons butter
1 teaspoon Frangelico liqueur❖ or vanilla extract
3 eggs
1 cup sugar
½ cup flour
½ tablespoon baking powder
¼ teaspoon salt
½ cup broken walnuts or pecans
One 3-ounce package cream cheese, softened
1 teaspoon vanilla extract

The Rolls-Royce of Brownies!

Preheat oven to 350°. Melt the chocolate and butter together in the top of a double boiler. In a bowl, using an electric mixer, beat Frangelico, 2 eggs, and ¾ cup of the sugar until thick and smooth.

In another bowl, stir together the flour, baking powder, and salt, and add to the egg mixture. Blend in the chocolate mixture and the nuts. Spread half the batter in a nonstick 9 × 13-inch pan.

Beat the remaining egg and sugar, the cream cheese, and the vanilla together; spread over the chocolate batter in the pan. Spread the remaining chocolate batter on top. With a knife, swirl through layers to marble. Bake 35 to 40 minutes. Test for doneness. When cool, cut into squares. Pack in a box, separated by layers of waxed paper, for the picnic.

❖ Frangelico was an Italian monk who lived as a hermit in the 16th century. He concocted this superb liqueur from wild hazelnuts, infused with berries and flowers and gave it his name. Its flavor is inimitable.

gala picnic

❖

champagne*
shrimp and prosciutto with jalapeño dip

country meat loaf
buttered rye bread*
green chili potato salad in potato skins

rodney's scotchies
fruit*

coffee in a thermos*

❖

*1986 Iron Horse Brut-Green Valley Sonoma,
Late Disgorged; and 1987 St. Francis Merlot,
Sonoma, are good wine choices.*

shrimp and prosciutto with jalapeño dip

24 medium shrimp,
 cooked, peeled, and
 deveined
¼ pound Prosciutto,
 sliced very thin and cut
 into strips 1 ½ × 3
 inches
Lemon and lime wedges,
 for garnish

Wrap each shrimp in a strip of Prosciutto and place, seam side down, on a platter that is to be transported to the picnic.

Garnish with wedges of lemon and lime. Cover with plastic wrap and chill for several hours, or overnight.

❧ jalapeño dip:

1 cup mayonnaise
2 teaspoons chopped
 green onion
1 teaspoon chopped fresh
 jalapeño
2 tablespoons ketchup
A few drops of lemon juice

Combine all ingredients in a bowl. Transfer to a plastic container with a lid. Store in a cooler to take to the picnic.

country meat loaf

1 ½ pounds meat loaf mix
 (1 pound ground beef,
 ¼ pound ground veal,
 ¼ pound ground pork
 or bulk pork sausage)
1 egg
2 slices homemade-style
 bread, soaked in
½ cup half-and-half
½ teaspoon salt
1 teaspoon red chili
 powder
1 tablespoon finely
 chopped onion
1 teaspoon chopped
 jalapeño pepper
1 teaspoon chopped fresh
 parsley
¼ cup fine bread crumbs
¼ cup (½ stick) butter,
 melted

Make this the night before the picnic.

Preheat oven to 350°. Combine all ingredients, except the bread crumbs and butter. Shape this mixture into a loaf and press into a 9 × 5 × 3-inch loaf pan. Sprinkle the bread crumbs over the loaf and pour the melted butter on top. Cover the pan with foil and bake for 45 minutes. Remove foil and bake another 15 minutes. Pour off juices and cool. Remove the meat loaf from the pan and wrap in heavy foil. Refrigerate overnight.

❧ buttered rye bread:

Butter rye bread slices on one side, form back into a loaf and wrap in foil.

Put chopped lettuce in a plastic bag. Take along a jar of Dijon mustard or honey mustard (or both), as well as a jar of sliced sweet pickles. And don't forget to take along a sharp knife to slice the meat loaf! Assemble the sandwiches at the picnic site. It's been said that many would "kill" for a meat loaf sandwich!

green chili potato salad in potato skins

6 large baking potatoes
3 tablespoons chopped onion
3 tablespoons chopped sweet pickles
½ cup chopped celery
1 hard-cooked egg, chopped
One 4-ounce can green chilies, chopped
½ teaspoon salt, or to taste
¼ teaspoon freshly ground pepper
2 tablespoons olive oil
1 tablespoon cider vinegar
½ cup mayonnaise
1 teaspoon prepared mustard
¼ cup chopped parsley, for garnish
½ cup piñon nuts, for garnish

Potato salad is best served at room temperature. The fresher it is, the more delicious. Make this as close to picnic time as possible.

Preheat oven to 400°. Wash the potatoes thoroughly. Pierce the top of each potato with the tines of a fork and bake for 1 hour. Remove from oven and cool until comfortable to handle.

Cut a thin slice from the top of each potato. With a spoon, carefully remove the pulp. Do not tear skins. Set skins aside. Dice the potato pulp. Add the onion, pickles, celery, egg, green chilies, salt, and pepper. To keep the texture, mix very carefully. You do not want mashed potatoes.

Add the oil and vinegar to the mixture. In a separate bowl, mix together the mayonnaise and mustard, and very, very gently combine with the potato mixture. Taste for seasoning. Divide and heap into reserved potato skins.

Garnish top of each potato with parsley and a sprinkle of piñon nuts. A cardboard bakery box is an excellent vehicle in which to transport this salad to the picnic. Keep it stored in a cooler until ready to serve.

rodney's scotchies

makes 12 to 15 squares

½ cup (1 stick) butter
1 cup brown sugar
1 egg
1 teaspoon Frangelico
    liqueur or vanilla extract
½ cup flour
1 teaspoon baking powder
½ teaspoon salt
1 cup chopped pecans

Preheat oven to 350°. Melt the butter. Mix in the brown sugar, and stir until sugar melts. Allow to cool for about 5 minutes. Beat the egg with the Frangelico and stir into butter-sugar mixture. Add the flour, baking powder, and salt. Mix well. Stir in the pecans and spread in a 10¾ × 7 × 1½-inch brownie pan. Bake for 20 to 25 minutes. Cut into squares when cool. Pack in a box separated by layers of waxed paper to take to the picnic.

picnic on the patio

For an unbelievably pleasurable occasion without leaving home, create a country atmosphere with a picnic on the patio or by the swimming pool. Fill a large napkin-lined basket with sandwiches made on several kinds of bread with a variety of fillings. Prepare a relish tray with pickled jalapeños, pitted ripe olives, large stuffed green olives, and strips of raw zucchini.

Choose either the Ambrosia Chicken Salad or Lobster Salad Fabulosa, or—as I once did—serve both for double the pleasure. This is a picnic you'll long remember!

❖

sandwich basket:
pilgrim's sandwich
olive-nut sandwich
egg salad sandwich
ambrosia chicken salad
or
lobster salad fabulosa

sicilian cake
or
chocolate charlotte russe cake

❖

This picnic pairs well with 1990 Joseph Phelps Vin du Mistral Grenache Rosé, California.

pilgrim's sandwich

6 ounces cooked turkey breast, chopped
½ cup mayonnaise
¼ cup cranberry-orange relish (Ocean Spray brand, for example)
1 tablespoon finely chopped green onion, white part only
2 tablespoons chopped pecans
Salt and pepper, to taste
8 slices sandwich bread
Butter
4 lettuce leaves
4 thin slices Swiss cheese

Combine the turkey, mayonnaise, relish, green onion, pecans, salt, and pepper. Remove crusts from the bread, and butter one side of each slice. Top 4 slices with a lettuce leaf. Divide turkey mixture evenly onto lettuce leaves. Cover each with a slice of cheese and one of the remaining bread slices.

Cut the sandwiches in half and wrap in plastic wrap to keep fresh until picnic time.

olive-nut sandwich

One 4½-ounce can chopped ripe olives
½ cup chopped pecans
Dash or two of Tabasco sauce
2 to 3 tablespoons mayonnaise
8 slices whole wheat bread

Combine the olives, pecans, Tabasco, and mayonnaise. Remove crusts from the bread and spread one side of each slice with softened butter. Top half the slices with filling and cover with the remaining slices of bread.

Cut into finger sandwiches.

egg salad sandwich

3 hard-cooked eggs, chopped
1 teaspoon chopped celery
¼ teaspoon dry mustard
Dash of Tabasco sauce
1½ tablespoons mayonnaise
Salt, to taste
Butter
12 slices party pumpernickel bread

Combine the eggs, celery, mustard, Tabasco, mayonnaise, and salt. Butter each slice of pumpernickel on one side. Spread half the slices of bread with the egg mixture. Cover with the remaining slices of bread.

Cut the sandwiches in half diagonally to make triangles.

ambrosia chicken salad

1 cup orange sections
(peel and slice oranges,
separate sections from
pith and membrane)
1 cup diced pineapple,
fresh or canned
1 cup sliced banana
½ cup chopped celery
1 ½ teaspoons salt
2 cups cooked, diced
chicken
¼ cup sliced black olives

Combine all salad ingredients in a large bowl. Set aside.

dressing:

¼ cup flour
3 tablespoons honey
½ teaspoon salt
¾ cup pineapple juice
2 egg yolks
¼ cup lemon juice
⅔ cup heavy cream,
whipped

Mix together the flour, honey, and salt in a 1-quart saucepan. Slowly add the pineapple juice. Mix well and cook over low heat until thickened.

In a separate bowl, beat the egg yolks and gradually stir in a small amount of the honey-pineapple juice mixture. Return to remaining mixture in the saucepan and cook for 2 or 3 minutes. Remove from heat and stir in the lemon juice. Combine with the chicken and fruit mixture.

Refrigerate until just before serving. Then fold in the whipped cream.

garnish:

Lettuce leaves
Watercress
½ cup broken walnuts
½ cup shredded coconut

Serve the salad on a platter lined with crisp lettuce leaves and garnished with watercress, walnuts, and coconut.

lobster salad fabulosa

1 tablespoon butter
1 tablespoon soy sauce
½ cup cashew nuts
½ cup piñon nuts
Chili powder, to taste
3 cups cooked lobster
    meat, broken into
    chunks
1 cup sliced celery
2 fresh jalapeño peppers,
    sliced
½ cup sliced green
    onions, white part only
One 5-ounce can sliced
    water chestnuts,
    drained
One 11-ounce can
    mandarin orange
    sections, drained
One 3-ounce can chow
    mein noodles

❦ dressing:

1 cup mayonnaise
¼ cup sour cream
¼ cup bottled chili sauce
1 teaspoon capers
½ teaspoon sugar
Salt, to taste

A combination of the Southwest and the Orient!

Melt the butter in a saucepan. Add the soy sauce and nuts. Stir constantly until nuts are lightly toasted. Remove from heat and set aside. Sprinkle lightly with chili powder.

Combine all remaining ingredients except the noodles in a large bowl. Gently fold in the chili-nut mixture, along with enough dressing (recipe follows) to moisten well. Sprinkle chow mein noodles on top. Serve remaining dressing on the side, to add if desired.

Gently mix all ingredients to blend.

sicilian cake

1 frozen pound cake about
9 inches long

This cake should be refrigerated overnight before serving.

Allow the cake to partially thaw. While thawing, prepare filling.

❧ filling:

1 pound ricotta cheese
1 cup sugar
1 cup mixed candied fruit,
coarsely chopped
2 ounces German's sweet
chocolate, chopped
½ ounce Strega liqueur

Beat the cheese until smooth. Fold in all other ingredients, except the pound cake. Set aside.

With a sharp knife, remove the brown crust from the sides and top of the cake. Slice lengthwise into at least 6 slices. Place bottom slice on a cake plate and spread generously with filling mixture. Place another slice on top, and repeat with more filling. Continue spreading each layer, ending with a plain slice of cake on top. Gently shape loaf with your hands. Refrigerate for an hour or two, then prepare the frosting.

❧ frosting:

Two 8-ounce squares
German's sweet
chocolate
¼ cup black coffee, plus 1
tablespoon instant
espresso granules
1 ½ cups (3 sticks)
unsalted butter, cut
into small pieces
½ ounce Strega liqueur

Melt the chocolate and coffee in the top of a double boiler, stirring constantly. Remove from heat. Add the butter and Strega. Beat until smooth.

Chill mixture until it thickens to spreading consistency. With a spatula, spread frosting over top and sides of the cake in decorative swirls. Chill overnight.

chocolate charlotte russe cake

This cake should rest overnight before serving.

1 cup semisweet chocolate
  morsels
2 tablespoons butter
One ¼-ounce envelope
  unflavored gelatin
2 tablespoons cold water
4 eggs, separated
¼ cup confectioners sugar
½ teaspoon orange-
  flavored extract
Pinch of salt
1 teaspoon freshly grated
  orange peel
1 tablespoon instant
  espresso coffee granules
1 tablespoon Grand
  Marnier
2 cups heavy cream
12 ladyfingers, split in
  half

In the top of a double boiler, melt the chocolate and butter over simmering water.

Soften the gelatin in the cold water and stir into the chocolate until dissolved. Remove from heat.

Add 1 egg yolk at a time to the chocolate mixture, stirring constantly with a wire whisk. Return to heat over simmering water. Add the sugar, orange extract, salt, orange peel, espresso granules, and Grand Marnier, and refrigerate. Whip cream until stiff. Reserve 1 cup of whipped cream for the top of the cake and fold remaining cream into the chilled chocolate mixture.

Line the bottom of a 9-inch spring form pan with 6 ladyfinger halves, split side facing up. Spread with ⅓ of the chocolate mixture. Cover with 6 more ladyfinger halves. Spread with ⅓ more of the chocolate mixture, followed by another 6 ladyfinger halves. Spread with remaining chocolate mixture, ending with 6 ladyfinger halves on top. Refrigerate overnight.

When ready to serve, remove from refrigerator, unlock spring on pan, and remove outer rim. Spread reserved whipped cream over cake and serve on a chilled platter.

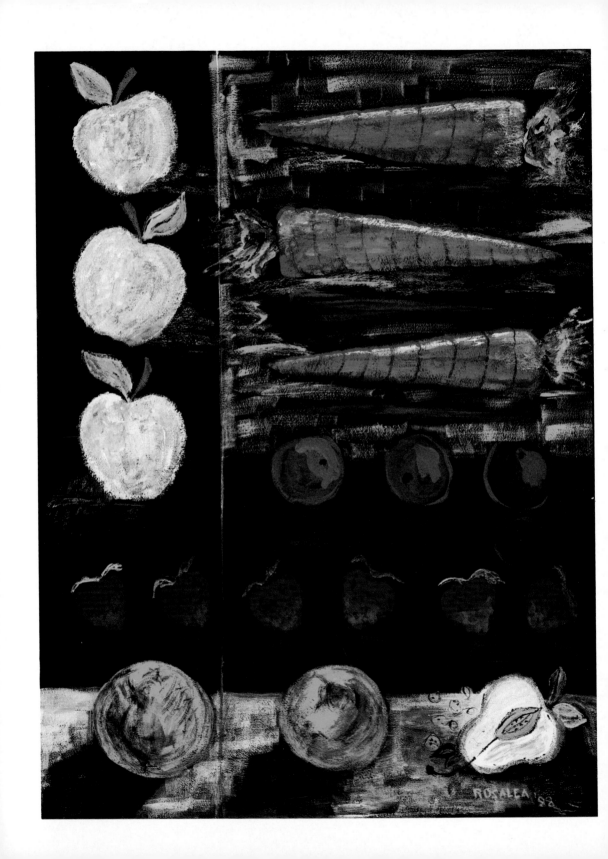

carefree picnic

❖

giant poor boy sandwich
barbequed drumsticks
salad of brown rice with peppers
hot spiced fruit

picnic apple loaf

❖

Quench your thirst with cold beer and apple cider.

giant poor boy sandwich

1 long loaf French bread
One 3-ounce package
  cream cheese, softened
3 or 4 tablespoons
  mayonnaise
Honey mustard
¼ pound cooked ham,
  sliced
¼ pound cooked turkey,
  sliced
¼ pound cooked pork or
  roast beef, sliced
¼ pound salami, sliced
¼ pound Swiss cheese,
  sliced
1 tomato, sliced
Sweet pickle slices
1 purple onion, sliced very
  thin
Chopped olives
Romaine lettuce leaves

Cut the bread in half lengthwise. Place the bottom half on a large piece of foil. Make a smooth paste of the cream cheese and mayonnaise. Spread both halves of the loaf with the cheese-mayonnaise mixture, then with mustard.

Arrange all the remaining ingredients on the bottom half of the loaf. Place the top half over the filling and cut the loaf diagonally into 6 pieces. Carefully bring foil around the loaf, folding the edges under to seal.

barbequed drumsticks

Salt and pepper
12 chicken drumsticks, 5
  to 6 ounces each
Flour
Vegetable oil, for frying

sauce:

¼ cup chopped onion
1 clove garlic, minced
2 ounces olive oil
¼ teaspoon Tabasco
  sauce
¼ cup lemon juice
2 tablespoons
  Worcestershire sauce
1 teaspoon sugar
2 teaspoons red chili
  powder
Pinch of oregano
1 cup water
½ cup ketchup

Preheat oven to 375°. Salt and pepper the drumsticks. Dredge in flour and brown in hot oil. When lightly browned, transfer to a baking pan.

In a heavy saucepan, sauté the onion and garlic in the olive oil until wilted. Add the remaining sauce ingredients. Cover and cook gently for 10 minutes. Add more water if necessary. Pour half the sauce over the drumsticks.

Cover and bake for about 30 minutes. Add remaining sauce and bake uncovered for 15 to 20 minutes.

When cool, cover with foil and take to picnic.

salad of brown rice with peppers

1 ½ cups brown rice
3 cups water
1 red bell pepper, cut into thin strips
1 yellow bell pepper, cut into thin strips
4 to 5 green onions, thinly sliced
½ cup pitted and chopped black olives
¼ cup chopped fresh parsley (reserve 1 teaspoon for garnish)
½ cup piñon nuts, for garnish

Place the rice and water in a medium saucepan. Bring to a boil, cover, and simmer until water is absorbed, 45 minutes to an hour.

While rice is cooking, prepare the dressing (recipe follows).

Pour dressing over warm rice and toss well. Taste for seasoning.

Add the peppers, onions, black olives, and parsley to the rice mixture and toss again.

Garnish with reserved parsley and the piñon nuts.

❧ dressing:

3 tablespoons balsamic vinegar
1 tablespoon Dijon mustard
½ teaspoon honey or sugar
¼ teaspoon salt
¼ teaspoon freshly ground black pepper
5 tablespoons olive oil

Combine all dressing ingredients in a mixing bowl. Cover bowl with plastic and take to picnic.

hot spiced fruit

One 8-ounce can pineapple chunks
One 8-ounce jar kumquats or mandarin oranges
One 8-ounce can apricot halves
¼ cup white vinegar
¼ cup brown sugar
½ cinnamon stick

Drain the pineapple, kumquats, and apricot halves, reserving ¼ cup syrup from each. In a saucepan, combine the ¾ cup syrup with the vinegar, brown sugar, and cinnamon stick. Bring to a boil. Reduce heat and simmer for 10 minutes. Add the fruit. Simmer for a few minutes more, until fruit is heated through.

picnic apple loaf

2 cups sugar
1 ½ cups vegetable oil
2 eggs, beaten
2 teaspoons Frangelico
liqueur or vanilla extract
3 cups cake flour
1 ½ teaspoons baking
powder
1 teaspoon salt
3 cups peeled, cored, and
chopped cooking apples
1 cup broken walnuts
1 cup white raisins

Preheat oven to 325°. Combine the sugar with the oil. Beat in the eggs and Frangelico. Fold in the flour, baking powder, and salt. When well mixed, add the chopped apples, nuts, and raisins.

Pour batter into a greased and floured 9 × 5 × 3-inch loaf pan. Bake for 1½ hours, or until a toothpick comes out clean when inserted into the center.

Allow cake to cool partially before removing from the pan. Glaze with Brown Sugar Glaze.

❧ brown sugar glaze:

2 tablespoons butter,
softened
½ cup brown sugar
2 tablespoons heavy
cream

Beat all ingredients together until smooth. Spread over warm cake.

Wrap in foil to transport.

barbeques

One of the most tantalizing aromas in the world is that of over-the-coals cooking. Outdoor cooking for fish and shellfish produces incomparable flavor, and the mouth-watering aroma of grilled meats has always been a special summertime delight.

The secret to cooking fish or shellfish is to never overcook it. Marinating your meat and fish before cooking will give the food a special piquant taste. I hope the recipes and tips offered here will enhance your reputation as a backyard chef.

All the menus are designed to serve 6 unless otherwise noted. Asterisks are used to indicate recipes that do not appear in this book.

barbequed ribs supreme

64

❖

shrimp on the barbie with roasted corn

68

❖

finger lickin' chicken barbeque

71

❖

old-fashioned hot dogs and beans

75

❖

tasty grilled salmon steaks

78

❖

festive ham and sweet potato barbeque

84

❖

barbequed ribs

supreme

❖

silver coin margaritas

joe boy's tequila supreme ribs
black-eyed peas with jalapeño
pink adobe coleslaw
garlic-buttered french bread

french peach pie

❖

silver coin margaritas

1 ounce Patron silver
  tequila
1 ounce Cointreau
Juice of 1 fresh lime
Juice of ½ fresh lemon
Juice of ¼ fresh orange
Splash of sweet-and-sour
  mix

makes 1 serving

Blend all ingredients together. Shake with ice. For serving in salt-rimmed glasses, follow directions for Margarita Gold (see page 19).

joe boy's tequila supreme ribs

David Wynne, a writer friend of mine, invented this method of preparing baby back ribs, that are by far the best I have ever tasted. Allow 2 hours preparation time before the barbeque.

6 pound rack of baby
  back ribs
1 cup tequila❖
1 cup water
Two 8-ounce bottles green
  chili salsa

In a wok or steamer, slowly steam the racks of ribs over the tequila and water for about 1 hour. Add more liquid if needed during steaming.

Remove the ribs from the steamer and cut into 2- or 3-rib portions. Preheat oven to 350°.

Place the ribs in an 8 × 15-inch baking pan. Cover with the green chili salsa. Cover with foil and bake for 1 hour.

When ready to serve, place the ribs on a grill over hot coals for about 5 minutes. Turn often to crisp edges.

❖ If you have drunk all of your tequila, substitute beer in the steaming process.

black - eyed peas with jalapeño

2 tablespoons olive oil
2 tablespoons chopped onion
1 tablespoon chopped green bell pepper
1 tablespoon (or more) chopped fresh jalapeño pepper
1 pound fresh black-eyed peas
1 small fresh tomato, chopped
Salt and pepper, to taste
Water

Heat the oil in heavy 2-quart saucepan. Sauté the onion, bell pepper, and jalapeño for a few minutes. Add the peas, tomato, salt, and pepper. Add water to cover and simmer until the peas are done, about 35 minutes or more. Test for doneness, and serve at once.

pink adobe coleslaw

1 medium head cabbage, finely shredded (4 cups)
⅓ cup chopped green onion
1 small unpeeled apple, cored and chopped
¾ cup pecans, chopped
¼ cup golden raisins
2 tablespoons sugar
Salt and pepper, to taste
3 tablespoons cider vinegar
¼ cup olive oil
½ cup sour cream
½ cup mayonnaise (or enough to moisten nicely)

In a large bowl, mix the cabbage, onion, apple, pecans, raisins, sugar, salt, and pepper. Add the vinegar and oil. Mix well. Add the sour cream and mayonnaise gradually, to achieve the consistency you prefer. This slaw should not be too wet.

garlic - buttered french bread

½ cup (1 stick) butter
1 small clove garlic, mashed
1 long loaf French bread, split in half lengthwise

Melt the butter with the garlic. Brush split sides of the loaf with butter mixture. Put halves together and wrap tightly in foil. Place on a hot grill; turn often, and watch carefully to avoid burning.

french peach pie

This is delicious served warm with a scoop of vanilla ice cream!

Preheat oven to 450°. To prepare the crust, work the flour, lard, and salt together with your fingers until crumbly. Add water just until dough holds together. Divide into two equal balls. On a floured pastry cloth, roll out one ball into a circle to line a 9-inch pie tin. Roll out second ball in same manner for the top crust.

To prepare the filling, place the peaches in the lined pie tin and sprinkle with the lemon juice, vanilla, nutmeg, and cinnamon. Spread the granulated sugar evenly over the peaches. In a bowl, mix the brown sugar and flour, and cut in the butter. When well blended, spread over peaches and sprinkle with the walnuts. Add most of the milk and cover with the top crust. Trim and crimp edges. Prick the top crust with a fork and brush the rest of the milk on the pastry.

Bake pie for 10 minutes, then reduce heat to 350° and bake for another 30 minutes. The crust should be golden when done.

❧ pastry:

2 cups flour
¾ cup lard
1 teaspoon salt
6 to 7 tablespoons water

❧ filling:

4 cups fresh peaches,
  peeled and sliced
2 tablespoons freshly
  squeezed lemon juice
1 teaspoon vanilla extract
½ teaspoon nutmeg
½ teaspoon cinnamon
½ cup granulated sugar
½ cup brown sugar
2 tablespoons flour
2 tablespoons butter
½ cup shelled, broken
  walnuts
¼ cup milk

shrimp on the barbie
with roasted corn

❖

hot cheese puffs

roasted corn
grilled shrimp
marinated vegetables

old-fashioned grasshopper pie

❖

1991 Caymus Sauvignon Blanc, Napa Valley,
goes well with this menu.

hot cheese puffs

8 to 10 slices white bread,
  crusts removed
½ cup (1 stick) butter
½ teaspoon Tabasco
  sauce
One 3-ounce package
  cream cheese
¼ cup shredded sharp
  Cheddar cheese
2 egg whites

Cut each slice of bread in quarters. Melt the butter in a 1-quart saucepan. Stir in the Tabasco and cheeses until soft and remove from heat. Beat the egg whites until stiff. Fold into cooled cheese mixture. Spread bread quarters with cheese mixture. Refrigerate for several hours.

Preheat oven to 400°. Bake about 15 minutes, until brown and puffed. Serve hot.

roasted corn

1 cup (2 sticks) butter,
  softened
1 teaspoon salt
½ teaspoon ground red
  chili powder
Pinch of oregano
Pinch of cumin
12 ears of corn on the
  cob, with husks

Cream the butter with the seasonings until fluffy. Turn back corn husks and remove silks. Spread the corn well with butter mixture and pull the husks back in position. Wrap each ear of corn in foil. Roast over hot coals, turning occasionally, for 15 to 20 minutes.

grilled shrimp

3 pounds jumbo shrimp
  (under 10 per pound)

❧ marinade:

¾ cup olive oil
¼ cup balsamic vinegar or
  white wine
¼ cup lemon juice
1 tablespoon
  Worcestershire sauce
Dash of Tabasco sauce
½ teaspoon salt
1 tablespoon bottled chili
  sauce
½ cup chopped onion
1 clove garlic, minced

Peel and devein the shrimp. Set aside.

To prepare the marinade, combine all ingredients. Pour over the shrimp. Cover with plastic wrap and marinate in the refrigerator for 3 to 4 hours. Drain shrimp and reserve marinade. Place shrimp in a well-greased wire grill basket. Grill over hot coals for 15 to 20 minutes, turning often and basting with marinade.

2 medium potatoes,
   peeled, cooked, and
   sliced
2 medium yellow squash,
   sliced
1 medium tomato, thinly
   sliced
1 small purple onion,
   peeled and thinly sliced
Salt and pepper
¾ cup olive oil
¼ cup balsamic vinegar
Chopped parsley, for
   garnish

marinated vegetables

Prepare the night before the barbeque.

Alternate layers of each vegetable in a glass bowl. Lightly salt and pepper each layer. Combine the oil and vinegar. Mix well. Pour over the vegetables, cover, and allow to marinate in the refrigerator for several hours, or overnight.

Garnish vegetables with parsley before serving.

❧ crust:

1 ½ cups cream-filled
   chocolate cookie crumbs
¼ cup (½ stick) butter,
   melted
½ cup pecans, chopped

❧ grasshopper filling:

Two ¼-ounce envelopes
   unflavored gelatin
¼ cup cold water
¼ cup freshly squeezed
   lime juice, heated to
   boiling
¼ cup white crème de
   cacao liqueur
½ cup crème de menthe
   liqueur
¼ cup sugar
2 egg whites, stiffly beaten
¾ cup heavy cream,
   whipped
3 squares semisweet
   chocolate, shaved

old-fashioned grasshopper pie

Expect many kudos when you revive the Grasshopper Pie. You won't regret taking the time to prepare this oldie.

Preheat oven to 370°. Combine the cookie crumbs, butter, and nuts and press firmly into the bottom and up the sides of a well-greased 9-inch pie pan. Bake for 7 minutes. Cool.

To prepare the filling, soften the gelatin in the cold water. Add the hot lime juice and stir until the gelatin is dissolved. Add the crème de cacao and crème de menthe, then the sugar. Stir until dissolved.

Chill until the mixture begins to set. Beat with a rotary beater until foamy. Fold in the egg whites, then the whipped cream. Turn into the baked cooled pie shell.

Sprinkle shaved chocolate over the top.

finger lickin' chicken barbeque

❖

marinated melon on skewers

barbequed lime chicken
zucchini with corn and green chilies
hot buttered french bread

lemon cloud pie

❖

*1990 Vichon Chevrignon, Napa Valley, pairs well with
this barbeque.*

1 ripe cantaloupe
1 ripe honeydew melon

marinated melon on skewers

☙ marinade:

½ cup freshly squeezed
  orange juice
¼ teaspoon grated orange
  rind
½ teaspoon grated lemon
  rind
¼ cup light corn syrup
¼ teaspoon vanilla extract
¼ teaspoon brandy
  (optional)

Remove flesh from the melons with a melon baller. Place the melon balls in a deep bowl. Mix marinade ingredients well and pour over the fruit. Cover and marinate in the refrigerator for 3 or 4 hours, turning carefully on occasion.

When ready to serve, alternate 3 or 4 cantaloupe and honeydew balls on wooden skewers. Serve at room temperature.

Three 3- to 3 ½-pound
  fryers, split in half

barbequed lime chicken

Marinate the night before the barbeque.

☙ marinade:

1 cup salad oil
1 cup freshly squeezed
  lime juice
1 tablespoon salt
1 teaspoon paprika
1 clove garlic, crushed
Dash of thyme, crushed
  in the palm of your
  hand

Place the chicken in shallow baking dishes. Combine marinade ingredients in an electric blender. Process until well blended. Pour marinade over chicken and cover tightly.

Marinate in the refrigerator overnight, turning a few times in the marinade.

Remove the chicken from the refrigerator about an hour before grilling. When ready to cook, drain chicken and reserve marinade. Place the chicken over hot coals and cook for about 20 minutes. Turn and cook for another 20 minutes, or until done. Brush often with marinade while grilling.

zucchini with corn and green chilies

(from *the pink adobe cookbook*)

¼ cup (½ stick) butter
1 tablespoon olive oil
½ cup chopped onion
½ cup chopped fresh
  green chilies
4 cups sliced zucchini, ½
  inch thick
1 ½ to 2 cups fresh corn
  kernels, scraped from
  about 4 ears
1 teaspoon salt
¼ teaspoon dried oregano
¼ teaspoon cumin seed
½ cup chicken or beef
  broth

Heat the butter and olive oil in a 12-inch skillet. Sauté the onion and green chilies for about 3 minutes. Add the zucchini, corn, salt, oregano, and cumin seed. Mix well. Stir in the broth.

Cover the skillet and simmer until the zucchini is crisp-tender, about 5 minutes. Serve hot.

hot buttered french bread

1 long loaf French bread,
  split in half lengthwise
½ cup (1 stick) butter,
  melted

Brush split sides of loaf with melted butter. Put halves together and wrap tightly in foil. Place on hot grill; turn often and watch carefully to avoid burning.

lemon cloud pie

This heavenly dessert can be prepared the night before.

pastry:

1 cup flour
½ teaspoon salt
*4 tablespoons butter or
vegetable shortening*
½ teaspoon vinegar
1 egg
*1 to 1 ½ tablespoons
water*

lemon cloud filling:

*One ¼-ounce envelope
unflavored gelatin*
¼ cup sugar
¼ teaspoon salt
1 cup water
*⅓ cup freshly squeezed
lemon juice*
2 egg yolks, beaten
*1 ½ teaspoons grated
lemon rind*
*2 cups heavy cream,
whipped*
*Very thin lemon slices, for
garnish*

Preheat oven to 400°. Sift the flour and salt together in bowl. Add the butter and, with a pastry blender or your hands, blend until mixture resembles coarse meal. Add the vinegar and egg. Mix well. Add water, a very little at a time, just until dough holds together.

Roll out the pastry on a floured surface. Place in a 9-inch pie pan. Crimp edges, prick sides and bottom with a fork. Bake about 15 minutes, until lightly browned. Let cool.

To prepare the filling, combine the gelatin, sugar, and salt in a heavy 2-quart saucepan. Add the water, lemon juice, and egg yolks. Blend well with a wire whisk. Cook for about 5 minutes over medium heat, stirring constantly until the gelatin dissolves. Remove from heat and stir in the lemon rind.

Turn into a large mixing bowl and chill until thickened. Beat with an electric beater until doubled in volume. Fold in the whipped cream and spoon filling into the cooled pie shell.

Chill for several hours, or overnight. Garnish with lemon slices before serving.

old-fashioned hot dogs and beans

❖

nostalgic hot dogs
roundup beans

french apple pie

❖

Serve with ice-cold beer and sodas.

sauce:

1 cup chopped onions
1 teaspoon finely chopped
   fresh jalapeño pepper
¼ cup sweet pickle relish
2 tablespoons finely
   chopped stuffed
   Spanish olives
½ cup ketchup
¼ cup prepared mustard
¼ cup mayonnaise
Salt and pepper
A few drops of Liquid
   Smoke

1 small head iceberg
   lettuce, finely chopped
1 large tomato, peeled and
   chopped
12 all-beef wieners (Ball
   Park brand are the
   best)
12 soft hot dog buns,
   buttered

nostalgic hot dogs

I call these nostalgic hot dogs because, after much experimenting, I think I have captured that haunting taste of hot dogs "the way they used to be." It is the sauce that evokes the memory.

Mix sauce ingredients together in a bowl.

In a bowl, mix together the lettuce and tomato.

Grill the wieners over hot coals until they puff and are lightly charred. Place in the buttered buns. Spread with a tablespoon or two of sauce. Sprinkle the lettuce and tomato mixture on top. Pass to guests.

roundup beans

2 cups dried pinto beans
1 small ham hock, 1 to
   2 ½ pounds
1 large onion, finely
   chopped
1 fresh jalapeño pepper,
   finely chopped
1 large green bell pepper,
   finely chopped
1 large clove garlic,
   minced
Salt and pepper, to taste

Soak the beans overnight. Drain and put in a large pot with all other ingredients. Cover with water and bring to a boil. Reduce heat and simmer for 1 hour. Remove the ham hock and pick meat from the bone. Discard the bone and return ham to the pot. Cook for 30 minutes more. Add a little water, if needed. The liquid should be thick.

When the beans are done, remove one cup to a small bowl. Mash and return to the pot. Mix well. Cook an additional 5 to 10 minutes.

french apple pie

pastry:

2 cups flour
¾ cup lard
1 teaspoon salt
6 to 7 tablespoons cold
water

apple filling:

1 pound fresh apples,
cored, peeled and sliced,
or one 16-ounce can
pie apples (not pie
filling)
2 tablespoons freshly
squeezed lemon juice
½ teaspoon nutmeg
½ teaspoon cinnamon
½ cup granulated sugar
¼ cup seedless raisins
1 cup brown sugar
2 tablespoons flour
2 tablespoons butter
½ cup shelled pecan
halves
¼ cup milk

hard sauce:

½ cup (1 stick) butter
1 ½ cups confectioners
sugar
1 tablespoon boiling water
1 teaspoon brandy or rum

(from *the pink adobe cookbook*)

This is the most popular dessert at The Pink Adobe. I have no idea how many French Apple Pies I've made—thousands, hundreds of thousands, maybe millions. At any rate, they've all been eaten with gusto.

Preheat oven to 450°. To prepare the crust, work the flour, lard, and salt together with your fingers until crumbly. Add water just until the dough holds together. Divide into 2 equal balls. On a floured pastry cloth, roll out one ball into a circle to line a 9-inch pie tin. Roll out the second ball in the same manner for the top crust.

Place the apples in the pastry-lined pie tin and sprinkle with the lemon juice, nutmeg, and cinnamon. Spread the granulated sugar and raisins evenly over the apples.

In a bowl, mix the brown sugar and flour, and cut in the butter. When well blended, spread over the apples and sprinkle with the pecans. Add most of the milk and cover with the top crust. Trim and crimp edges. Prick the top crust with a fork and brush with the rest of the milk.

Bake for 10 minutes, then reduce heat to 350° and bake another 30 minutes. The crust should be golden brown. Serve warm, with Hard Sauce (recipe follows).

Cream the butter until fluffy. Beat in the sugar and water, then the liquor.

tasty grilled salmon steaks

❖

honeydew melon with lime wedges*

grilled salmon steaks
carrot, potato, green chili, and olive salad
herb-buttered french bread

chocolate-piñon cookies with orange glaze

❖

1990 Flora Springs Chardonnay, Napa Valley, Barrel Fermented, is very good with these salmon steaks.

grilled salmon steaks

Six 5- to 6-ounce salmon
steaks, 1-inch thick
½ cup olive oil
¼ cup freshly squeezed
lemon or lime juice
2 tablespoons grated
onion
1 teaspoon Dijon mustard
¼ cup chopped parsley
¼ teaspoon salt
¼ teaspoon freshly
ground pepper

Place the salmon in a shallow dish or a plastic bag. Combine all other ingredients and pour marinade over fish. Marinate overnight in the refrigerator.

When ready to grill, drain the salmon and reserve marinade. Place fish in a well-greased wire grill basket. Grill over medium-hot coals for 6 to 8 minutes. Turn over, baste with marinade, and grill for another 6 to 8 minutes, or until the salmon flakes when tested with a fork.

Serve tartar sauce on the side, if desired.

carrot, potato, green chili, and olive salad

3 cups diced carrots
2 cups diced white pota-
toes
1 tablespoon butter
¼ cup chopped green
onion
1 cup large pitted ripe
olives, cut in quarters
One 4-ounce can chopped
green chilies
½ cup Blue Cheese
Dressing (recipe
follows)
Watercress, olives, carrot
curls, for garnish

In boiling salted water, cook the carrots and potatoes until just tender, about 5 minutes. Do not overcook. Melt the butter in a small skillet. Sauté the green onion for a few minutes. Mix the carrots and potatoes with the green onions. Add the olives and green chilies and mix. Lightly stir in the dressing and press mixture into a well-greased 8-cup mold. Cover and refrigerate overnight.

When ready to serve, unmold onto a serving platter and garnish with watercress, olives, and carrot curls.

❧ blue cheese dressing:

⅔ cup olive oil
⅓ cup lemon juice
1 teaspoon salt
¼ teaspoon pepper
½ teaspoon paprika
½ teaspoon sugar
2 tablespoons blue cheese

makes just over 1 cup dressing

Place all ingredients in a food processor or blender and process until well blended.

herb-buttered french bread

1 long loaf French bread
¼ cup (½ stick) butter,
   softened
1 tablespoon chopped
   parsley
1 tablespoon honey
   mustard
Pinch of savory
Pinch of celery seed

Slice the bread diagonally, about 1 inch thick. Do not cut through the bottom crust. Mix the butter with the seasonings and spread between slices of bread.

Wrap the loaf in heavy-duty foil and place on the edge of grill. Heat for about 15 minutes, turning frequently.

chocolate-piñon cookies with orange glaze

makes 50 to 60 cookies

1 cup (2 sticks) butter
¼ cup sugar
1 teaspoon vanilla extract
⅔ cup grated semisweet
   chocolate
1 cup piñon nuts
2¼ cups cake flour
½ teaspoon salt

Preheat oven to 350°. With an electric mixer, cream the butter and sugar. Stir in the vanilla, grated chocolate, and piñon nuts. Mix in the flour and salt. Chill the dough.

When ready to bake, roll out the dough ⅛ inch thick on a floured pastry cloth. Cut out cookies with a 2–3-inch round cookie cutter. Place slightly apart on a nonstick cookie sheet.

Bake 10 minutes, or until cookies are dry and firm. When cool, brush with a thin coating of Orange Glaze (recipe follows).

❧ orange glaze:

1 cup orange marmalade
2 to 4 tablespoons orange-
   flavored brandy, such
   as Grand Marnier

Heat the marmalade in a heavy saucepan, stirring constantly, until it is boiling. Stir in the brandy. Use the glaze while it is hot.

festive ham and sweet potato barbeque

❖

ham steaks with ginger-peach marmalade glaze
grilled sweet potatoes
layered fruit salad
hot buttered french bread (see page 73)

pecan loaf

❖

*Serve 1990 Matanzas Creek Chardonnay, Sonoma, to enhance
the flavors of this barbeque.*

ham steaks with ginger-peach marmalade glaze

2 center-cut, fully cooked
  ham steaks, 1 ½ inches
  thick

❧ glaze:

One 16-ounce jar ginger-
  peach marmalade
2 tablespoons prepared
  mustard
2 teaspoons freshly
  squeezed lemon juice
1 tablespoon water

Cut slashes in the fat around the edges of the ham to prevent curling during grilling. Place the ham in a shallow dish.

In a 1-quart saucepan, combine the marmalade, mustard, lemon juice, and water. Stir over low heat until marmalade melts. Pour the glaze over the ham, cover, and refrigerate overnight, or let stand at room temperature for at least 2 hours. When ready to grill, drain the ham and reserve glaze.

Grill the ham over medium coals for 15 minutes, brushing occasionally with glaze. Turn and grill for another 10 to 15 minutes. Heat the remaining reserved glaze in a saucepan on the edge of the grill. Slice the ham steaks to serve and pass the heated glaze separately.

grilled sweet potatoes

6 medium unpeeled sweet
   potatoes or yams
Olive oil
Butter
Salt and pepper, to taste

Start grilling these at least half an hour before the ham is cooked. Start your coals early. They can be done directly on the coals, if desired.

Scrub the potatoes and dry well. Rub with oil and wrap each potato in a square of foil. Seal tightly by overlapping the edges. Grill for 1 hour, turning frequently.

When ready to serve, slit the foil, cut a cross in the potato and push ends to fluff. Put a pat of butter in each potato and season with salt and pepper.

layered fruit salad

1 cup strawberries, stems
   removed, halved
1 cup fresh pineapple
   chunks
1 cup canteloupe or
   honeydew melon balls
1 medium banana, sliced
One 8-ounce carton of
   strawberry-banana
   yogurt (or the flavor of
   your choice)

In a glass bowl, layer the fruit, spreading each layer with 4 tablespoons of the yogurt. Cover and chill for several hours.

pecan loaf

1 cup (2 sticks) butter
1 cup sugar
6 eggs
1 teaspoon vanilla extract
2 cups flour
2 teaspoons baking pow-
  der
1 teaspoon grated orange
  peel
½ cup milk
3 cups broken pecan
  pieces
Confectioners sugar

Preheat oven to 350°. Grease and lightly flour a 9 × 5 × 3-inch loaf pan.

With an electric mixer, cream the butter and sugar together until fluffy. Add the eggs, one at a time, beating well after each addition. Add the vanilla. Mix again. Sift together the flour and baking powder; add the orange peel. Add the flour mixture to the creamed mixture, alternating with the milk. Stir in the nuts.

Pour into the prepared loaf pan and bake 50 to 60 minutes, or until the cake tests done. (When a toothpick is inserted in the center and comes out clean, or when the cake pulls away from the pan, it is done.) Cool in the pan. Remove and dust the cake with confectioners sugar before serving.

cocktail parties

The cocktail party is one of the most seductive and popular ways to entertain. It is the most festive of get-togethers and can provide a wonderful opportunity to be creative. Much of the preparation can be done ahead of time. Thought should be given to the visual appeal of the trays. The colors should always be compatible, and by all means consider the textures. Don't bore your guests with a completely smooth, creamy taste throughout. Add crunch and snap with nuts, raw vegetables, and water chestnuts; add zest with chili and seasonings.

Appetizers can be elaborate or simple. It is the ingenious presentation that can result in a dramatic display. Be daring with shapes: either for the canapés themselves or the platters and plates they are served on. A tray decorated with a few fresh flowers can be seriously appetite provoking and will create an aura of restrained elegance.

Ice sculpture achieves a lovely effect, but if this is not your talent, try this easy method of making colored ice molds. Into a round mold or a straight-sided bowl, pour water that has been tinted with a few drops of food coloring. Place a glass bowl in the center and freeze. When the mold is removed, the glass bowl will be frozen into the ice. Place the ice on a platter that will catch the drippings. Surround with a wreath of watercress or other greens. Fill the bowl with seafood.

Asterisks are used to indicate recipes that are not included in this book.

an informal gathering for friends

For a small informal gathering, this is a classic Santa Fe crowd pleaser. Serve a simple green salad, if desired, and ice cream for dessert. Better yet, serve Häagan-Dazs chocolate fudge ice cream bars. You are sure to be rewarded with squeals of delight!

❖

santa fe layered mashed beans with
chorizo and chips
jalapeño salsa (see page 13)

häagan-dazs chocolate fudge ice cream bars*

❖

Rosalitas (page 15) or Margaritas, and cold Corona Extra are perfect accompaniments to this cocktail party.

santa fe layered mashed beans with chorizo and chips

3 cups cooked pinto beans
¼ cup minced onion
1 clove garlic, mashed
1 cup shredded sharp
  Cheddar cheese
6 (or more) drops Tabasco
  sauce
2 pickled jalapeño
  peppers, minced
Salt, to taste
4 tablespoons bacon or
  ham fat
1 ½ cups crumbled
  chorizo❖
Chopped pitted ripe olives,
  for garnish
Chopped parsley, for
  garnish
2 large bags tortilla chips

Drain and mash the beans, or put them through a food mill. Add the onion, garlic, cheese, Tabasco, jalapeños, and salt. Heat the fat in a large skillet and add the bean mixture. Stir until the cheese is melted and the whole mixture is bubbling. Set aside.

In a separate skillet, brown the chorizo, stirring and turning often.

To assemble, mound the bean mixture on a large platter. Spread the browned chorizo on top. Garnish with olives and parsley. Arrange the chips around the platter, sticking some into the bean mixture. Serve the Jalapeño Salsa on the side.

Combine all ingredients well.

1 pound ground pork
  sausage
2 tablespoons powdered
  red chili
¼ teaspoon oregano
¼ teaspoon ground cumin
1 clove garlic, crushed
Dash each: cinnamon
  and nutmeg

❖ Chorizo is a Mexican sausage. Remove from the casing to crumble. Chorizo is available in most markets, but if you are unable to find it, you can easily prepare your own:

easy and elegant cocktails

The menu for this small party is a simple and harmonious selection of foods that complement one another. Most of the preparation can be done well in advance. The meatballs can be mixed, shaped, and refrigerated overnight. The smoked salmon cheesecake can be made the day before. Have the food ready and placed at different stations before your guests arrive.

The Chili-Honey Pecans and Celery with Caviar should be served in small bowls placed on various tables, where they will be easily accessible to guests sitting or standing around the room. Place the chafing dish at some distance from the Smokey Salmon Cheesecake and Chinese Minced Chicken and Lettuce Leaves.

This arrangement will keep guests moving easily, and will disperse the small clusters of 2 or 3 people that usually form at small cocktail parties. Toward the end of the evening, set out the Date-Walnut Bars, coffee, and brandy on a table for self-service.

❖

chili-honey pecans
celery with caviar
smokey salmon cheesecake squares
chinese minced chicken in lettuce leaves
chafing dish meatballs with green chili mayonnaise

date-walnut bars

❖

*Veuve Clicquot Ponsardin, 1991 Caymus
"Conundrum," and 1988 Carneros Creek Pinot Noir
are excellent wine choices.*

chili-honey pecans

½ cup hot oil (available in
    Oriental section of
    supermarket)
2 tablespoons red chili
    powder
¼ teaspoon ground cumin
1 teaspoon salt
3 tablespoons honey
4 cups pecan halves

Preheat oven to 350°. Combine the hot oil, chili powder, cumin, salt, and honey in a skillet. When hot, remove from the heat and stir in the pecans until well coated. Place pecans on a baking sheet and roast for 10 to 15 minutes, or until crisp. Stir and shake frequently, as they can brown quickly. Add more salt if necessary.

Place in small bowls and serve.

One 3-ounce package
    cream cheese
2 tablespoons sour cream
¼ teaspoon grated onion
Salt and pepper, to taste
1 teaspoon freshly
    squeezed lemon juice
thirty 2-inch-long pieces of
    celery,
One 2-ounce jar caviar

celery with caviar

Beat the cream cheese and sour cream together until smooth. Add the onion, salt, pepper, and lemon juice. Stuff the celery with this mixture. Top each piece of celery with a dab of caviar.

smokey salmon cheesecake squares

An easy and elegant appetizer.

1 ½ cups crumbled saltine crackers❖ (about 25)

1 cup pecans, coarsely chopped

Two 8-ounce packages cream cheese

1 cup ricotta cheese

¼ cup heavy cream or canned evaporated milk

2 eggs

1 tablespoon finely chopped onion

2 fresh jalapeño peppers, finely chopped

One 15 ½-ounce can red sockeye salmon, drained and flaked

½ teaspoon Liquid Smoke

Chopped parsley, for garnish

Preheat oven to 350°. Sprinkle the crumbled saltines evenly over the bottom of a 9½ × 13-inch nonstick baking pan. Spread the pecans evenly over the crushed crackers.

With an electric mixer set on medium speed, beat the cream cheese, ricotta, cream, eggs, onion, and jalapeños until smooth. Fold the salmon and Liquid Smoke into the cheese mixture. Spoon into the pan and smooth the top.

Bake 40 to 45 minutes, or until a toothpick inserted in the center comes out clean. Let cool in pan. Invert onto a cookie sheet and cut into 2-inch squares. Arrange on a serving platter and garnish with parsley.

❖ To crumble the saltines, place them in a plastic bag and squeeze with your hands.

chinese minced chicken in lettuce leaves

1 or 2 large heads of
 iceberg lettuce
¼ cup vegetable oil
6 cups minced cooked
 chicken
2 green onions, minced
12 black mushrooms,
 presoaked❖ and
 minced
1 cup water chestnuts,
 minced
3 tablespoons minced
 gingerroot
1 tablespoon oyster
 sauce❖❖
1 tablespoon soy sauce
½ teaspoon sugar
1 teaspoon sesame oil

Wash the lettuce. Remove and separate the leaves and cut in half. Wrap in a towel and place in the refrigerator to crisp.

Heat the vegetable oil in a large skillet or wok. Add the chicken and green onions and stir-fry briefly. Stir in the remaining ingredients and continue to stir-fry until well blended. Do not overcook. Place in a serving bowl.

At serving time, arrange lettuce leaves on a platter next to the bowl of Chinese Minced Chicken. Each guest puts a bit of the chicken mixture on a lettuce leaf, folds it, and eats out of hand. This should be served at room temperature.

❖ To presoak mushrooms: Soak in lukewarm water for about 2 hours, then squeeze dry. In fresh lukewarm water, soak again, overnight. Drain.

❖❖ Oyster sauce is available in the Oriental section of supermarket.

chafing dish meatballs with green chili mayonnaise

makes 40 to 45 small meatballs

½ cup heavy cream
¾ cup saltine cracker
    crumbs
1 ½ pounds ground beef
½ pound ground pork
1 teaspoon dried basil
1 teaspoon salt
3 tablespoons grated
    onion
¼ teaspoon cayenne
1 egg
3 tablespoons butter, for
    sautéing

In a bowl, mix the cream with the cracker crumbs and set aside. Make sure all the crumbs are moistened. In another bowl, mix the beef, pork, and other ingredients, except the butter, together. Add the crumb mixture to the meat and blend well. Shape into 1-inch meatballs. Cover and refrigerate overnight.

When ready to cook, melt the butter in a frying pan. Sauté the meatballs, turning often to brown all sides. Add more butter as needed. Transfer to a chafing dish. Provide cocktail picks for spearing, and serve with Green Chili Mayonnaise (recipe follows) on the side.

2 cups mayonnaise
¼ cup sour cream
6 green chilies, roasted,
    peeled, stems removed,
    and chopped, or one
    4-ounce can chopped
    green chilies
1 tablespoon lime juice
¼ teaspoon fresh cilantro
¼ teaspoon sugar
¼ teaspoon ground cumin
Salt, to taste
Chopped fresh jalapeño
    pepper, to taste, if a
    hotter dip is desired

green chili mayonnaise:

Mix all ingredients together until well blended.

date-walnut bars

½ cup (1 stick) butter
1 cup sugar
2 egg yolks (reserve whites for Date-Walnut Mixture)
1 ½ cups flour
1 teaspoon baking powder
Pinch of salt
½ teaspoon Frangelico liqueur or vanilla extract

Preheat oven to 350°. Cream together the butter and sugar. Add the egg yolks and beat well. Sift together the flour, baking powder, and salt. Add the dry ingredients to the butter mixture and mix until all the flour is incorporated. Stir in the Frangelico. Spread the batter into greased 9 × 13-inch pan. Set aside.

❧ date-walnut mixture:

2 egg whites
1 cup brown sugar
1 cup broken walnuts
1 cup chopped dates
½ teaspoon Frangelico liqueur or vanilla extract

Beat the egg whites until stiff. Add the brown sugar, walnuts, dates, and Frangelico. Mix gently but well. Spread carefully over the batter in the pan. Bake 40 to 45 minutes. When cool, cut into squares.

a cocktail buffet

serves 18 to 20

Combining the cocktail hour with an early supper is an easy and elegant way of entertaining. The opportunities for "mixing and matching" are endless. Since the seating arrangements at these affairs are usually very informal, I have chosen a menu that requires only forks.

All the food for this buffet can be prepared ahead of time, except for the last-minute broiling of the mushrooms and baking of the cheese balls. The brisket should be marinated the night before. The morning of the party, start cooking the brisket, make the horseradish sauce, and assemble the noodle casserole. The caviar eggs can be prepared several hours before the party, and the mushrooms can be prestuffed—ready for the last few minutes under the broiler

Have the bar situated well away from the buffet table in order to avoid traffic jams.

❖

drinks
open bar, including nonalcoholic drinks
white lillet with a splash of campari, a spritz of
seltzer, and a twist of lemon

appetizers to be passed on trays
pecan stuffed mushrooms
caviar stuffed eggs
bacon and cheddar cheese balls

on buffet table
brisket of beef with thin-sliced rye or pumpernickel
bread and horseradish sauce
buttered noodle casserole

dessert
tomato preserve cookies

❖

A *1989 Chimney Rock Fumé Blanc, Stag's Leap
District, and a 1986 Sequoia Grove Cabernet Sauvignon, Estate
Bottled, would be excellent wine choices for this buffet.*

pecan stuffed mushrooms

40 whole fresh
mushrooms
3 to 4 tablespoons olive oil
1 small onion
1 cup pecan pieces
4 tablespoons butter
A dash of thyme
⅓ cup bread crumbs
¼ teaspoon Tabasco
sauce
1 teaspoon Worcestershire
sauce
½ teaspoon salt
⅓ cup freshly grated
Parmesan cheese

Remove the stems from the mushrooms and rub the caps with olive oil. Chop the mushroom stems, onion, and pecans coarsely. In a large skillet, melt the butter and sauté the stem-pecan mixture for 5 minutes. Add the thyme, bread crumbs, Tabasco, Worcestershire, and salt.

Place the caps on a baking sheet and broil for 2 minutes on each side—watch carefully. Let the caps cool a few minutes, then fill with the crumb mixture.

Just before serving, sprinkle with the Parmesan and place under the broiler for a few minutes, until heated through.

caviar stuffed eggs

15 hard-cooked eggs
2 tablespoons minced,
green onion, white part
only
3 tablespoons mayonnaise
½ teaspoon freshly
squeezed lemon juice
¼ teaspoon salt
4 or 5 drops Tabasco
sauce
¼ teaspoon dry mustard
Sour cream
One 2-ounce jar black
caviar

Slice the eggs in half lengthwise and remove the yolks to a bowl. Mix the yolks with the onion, mayonnaise, lemon juice, salt, Tabasco, and mustard. Add a little more mayonnaise if the mixture seems too dry. Divide mixture evenly among the egg-white halves. Spread a little sour cream over each filled half and dab with caviar.

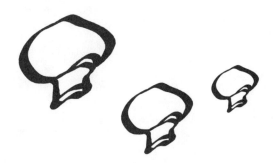

bacon and cheddar cheese balls

½ pound sharp Cheddar cheese, softened at room temperature for an hour or overnight
½ cup butter, softened
1 cup flour
½ cup crisply cooked, crumbled bacon
Paprika or chili powder, to dust

Preheat oven to 350°. Combine cheese and butter in a blender to mix. Slowly add the flour. Remove from the blender and add the bacon bits. Form into walnut-size balls. Dust with paprika or chili powder. Refrigerate until thoroughly chilled. Place on a baking sheet and bake for 10 to 15 minutes, until the bottoms are lightly browned. Serve hot.

brisket of beef with thin-sliced rye or pumpernickel bread and horseradish sauce

One 6- to 7-pound brisket
  of beef
¼ cup brown sugar
2 teaspoons salt
1 teaspoon freshly ground
  black pepper
One 10-ounce bottle chili
  sauce
1 ½ cups cider vinegar
½ cup olive oil
2 cups celery leaves,
  chopped
2 large onions, sliced
1 fresh jalapeño pepper,
  chopped

Place the meat in a shallow baking dish. Combine the brown sugar, salt, pepper, chili sauce, vinegar, and oil in a bowl and pour over the meat. Cover and refrigerate overnight.

Preheat oven to 325°. Transfer the meat to a roasting pan. Pour the marinade over the meat. Top with the celery leaves, onion, and jalapeño. Cover the pan and roast the meat for 1 hour per pound, or until tender. Uncover for the last hour of cooking. When ready to serve, remove the meat from the pan. Strain pan juices and return to pan. Slice the meat and reheat in strained juices. Serve with sliced rye or pumpernickel bread and Horseradish Sauce (recipe follows).

horseradish sauce:

1 cup sour cream
½ cup mayonnaise
1 teaspoon salt
2 teaspoons freshly
  squeezed lemon juice
½ cup prepared white
  horseradish sauce
1 teaspoon very finely
  chopped onion

Combine all ingredients in a mixing bowl. Chill for an hour or so for the flavors to blend.

buttered noodle casserole

Two 16-ounce packages
wide egg noodles,
cooked according to
package directions
1 ½ cups butter, melted
½ cup freshly grated
Parmesan cheese
½ cup freshly grated
Romano cheese
Two 10-ounce packages
frozen green peas
½ cup bread crumbs
1 tablespoon red pepper
flakes

Preheat oven to 375°. Mix the cooked noodles with 1 cup of the melted butter, the Parmesan and Romano cheeses, and the frozen peas. Place in a 4-quart casserole. Mix the bread crumbs and pepper flakes with the remaining butter. Sprinkle over the noodles and bake 10 to 15 minutes, until bubbly. Serve hot.

tomato preserves cookies

❧ cream cheese
pastry:

One 6-ounce package
cream cheese
½ pound butter
2 cups flour
3 tablespoons sugar
¼ teaspoon salt

Cut the cream cheese and butter into the flour. Add the sugar and salt. Blend well. Roll into a ball, wrap in waxed paper, and refrigerate overnight.

Preheat oven to 400°. Roll out the pastry to ⅛-inch thickness. Cut into 2-inch squares and place one teaspoon preserves on each square. Fold into triangles and pinch edges together. Place the cookies on an ungreased cookie sheet. Brush with milk and bake for 10 to 12 minutes. Cool on a wire rack.

One 10-ounce jar tomato
preserves
Milk, to brush cookies

fabulous finger foods

serves 20

❖

assorted nuts*
chili-crab crispies
gruyère french toast squares
pickled shrimp with caviar sauce or
chili dunking sauce
piñon chicken balls

fresh fruit*

❖

*Schramsberg Blanc de Noirs, 1990 Vichon Chevrignon, and
1988 Stag's Leap Winery Merlot are good
wine selections.*

chili-crab crispies

6 Old El Paso Tostada
Shells

❧ chili-cheese
mixture:

One 3-ounce package
cream cheese
1 tablespoon minced green
onion, white part only
1 tablespoon minced fresh
jalapeño pepper
¼ teaspoon salt
One 4-ounce can Old El
Paso chopped green
chilies, well drained
1 cup lump crab meat or
one 6½-ounce can
white crab meat, well
drained

❧ topping:

½ can Old El Paso
tomatoes and jalapeños
½ cup shredded Gruyère
cheese

I invented this recipe for the Old El Paso Food Company. They used it in a national advertising campaign.

Assemble all ingredients before starting.

Preheat oven to 350°. Break each tostada shell into 4 pieces. Place on a cookie sheet and brown in the oven for 5 minutes. Leave on the cookie sheet and set aside.

While browning the tostadas, prepare the Chili-Cheese Mixture.

Mash the cream cheese in a bowl to soften. Mix in the green onion, jalapeño, salt, and green chilies. Gently stir in the crab meat without mashing it.

Divide the Chili-Cheese Mixture among the tostada pieces. Top each with a dollop of tomatoes and jalapeños. Sprinkle with the Gruyère.

Put under the broiler until the cheese melts—2 to 3 minutes. Watch carefully! Use a spatula to loosen the crispies from the cookie sheet. Serve hot.

gruyère french toast squares

16 slices thin-sliced white
   bread
½ to 1 cup (1 to 2 sticks)
   butter, plus additional
   for bread
8 thin slices Gruyère
   cheese
1 cup milk
3 eggs

Remove crusts from the bread; lightly butter one side of each slice. Place a slice of cheese on half the slices of bread and top with the remaining bread. Press the sandwiches together firmly. Beat the milk and eggs together until well blended. Dip the sandwiches in this mixture. Set aside.

In a large skillet, heat ¼ cup of the butter. Fry 2 or 3 sandwiches at a time, turning and pressing with a spatula until the cheese is melted and the bread is nicely browned on both sides. Add more butter to the skillet as needed.

Cut each sandwich into 4 squares and serve immediately.

2 pounds small raw
    shrimp
⅔ cup cider vinegar
4 tablespoons olive oil
1 cup dry vermouth
2 tablespoons sugar
2 tablespoons salt
2 tablespoons pickling
    spice, in a bag or
    wrapped in cheesecloth
2 small onions, cut in half

❧ caviar sauce:

Two 2-ounce jars lumpfish
    caviar
2 cups sour cream
2 tablespoons lemon juice

❧ chili dunking
    sauce:

3 cups sour cream
1 ½ cups mayonnaise
4 fresh green chilies,
    chopped, or two
    4-ounce cans green
    chilies
2 teaspoons chopped
    green onion, white part
    only
½ teaspoon minced garlic

1 cup finely chopped
    cooked chicken
½ teaspoon finely
    chopped green onion,
    white part only
½ cup Brie cheese
2 teaspoons salt
½ teaspoon Tabasco
    sauce
2 to 4 tablespoons
    Madeira wine
1 cup piñon nuts, finely
    chopped

pickled shrimp with caviar sauce or chili dunking sauce

Peel and devein the shrimp. Put the remaining ingredients in a 3-quart saucepan. Add the shrimp, bring to a slow boil, and simmer for 2 minutes. Do not overcook or the shrimp will be tough. Cool the shrimp in the liquid. Drain the shrimp and serve warm or at room temperature, with toothpicks and Caviar Sauce or Chili Dunking Sauce on the side.

Mix all ingredients for the caviar sauce together. Serve at once or refrigerate until needed.

Mix all ingredients for the chili dunking sauce together to blend well. Refrigerate several hours before using.

piñon chicken balls

Combine all ingredients except the nuts. Use a small melon baller or spoon to scoop the mixture into balls. Roll the chicken balls in the piñon nuts and chill until firm. Spear with frilled cocktail picks to serve.

a cocktail cornucopia

serves 20

❖

peppered beef with green peppercorn sauce
thinly sliced rye bread*
big easy
artichoke leaves with shrimp
crab mousse with caviar cream
lobster, shrimp, and chicken salad

chocolate meringue puffs

❖

*Serve Domaine Chandon Brut; 1988 St. Francis Chardonnay,
Barrel Select; and 1988 Newton Claret.*

peppered beef with green peppercorn sauce

¼ to ½ cup coarsely
  ground black pepper
One 4- to 5-pound beef
  tenderloin

❧ marinade:

½ cup soy sauce
¼ cup red wine
2 tablespoons honey
1 teaspoon paprika
1 clove garlic, crushed

Spread pepper on a large sheet of waxed paper and roll the tenderloin in the pepper. Cover all sides and the ends, pressing the pepper into the meat with the heel of your hand. Mix all marinade ingredients together. Place the beef in the marinade, cover, and refrigerate overnight.

When ready to cook, preheat oven to 400°. Drain off the marinade. Wrap the beef in foil and roast in a baking dish for 20 to 30 minutes, or until the internal temperature reaches 120° for rare. Unwrap and place the beef under the broiler for a minute or two to brown. Slice thin and serve with Green Peppercorn Sauce (recipe follows) and thinly sliced rye bread on the side.

❧ green peppercorn sauce:

2 tablespoons chopped
  shallots
1 tablespoon butter
1 tablespoon green
  peppercorns, crushed
½ cup red wine vinegar
2 tablespoons cognac
½ cup beef bouillon
2 cups heavy cream
2 tablespoons prepared
  white horseradish
Salt, to taste

Sauté the shallots in the butter until golden brown. Add the peppercorns, vinegar, and cognac. Boil to reduce to ¼ cup, about 4 minutes. Add the beef bouillon and cream. Boil until reduced to a thick sauce, about 5 minutes. Mix in the horseradish and season with salt.

big easy
(a new orleans favorite)

Fifteen ½-inch slices
  French bread
¾ cup (1 ½ sticks) butter,
  softened
½ pound Roquefort
  cheese
½ cup walnuts, coarsely
  chopped
Pinch of cayenne
Dash of Tabasco sauce

Trim crusts from the bread and butter one side of each slice with ½ stick of the butter. Cut the bread into 1-inch-wide strips. Combine the cheese, remaining butter, walnuts, cayenne, and Tabasco. Lightly toast the bread strips on the buttered side. Spread the cheese mixture generously on the unbuttered side and broil briefly, until brown.

artichoke leaves with shrimp

makes 40 or more appetizers

2 or 3 large artichokes
1 teaspoon olive oil
Two 3-ounce packages
  cream cheese
¼ teaspoon Tabasco
  sauce
¼ teaspoon salt
3 tablespoons heavy
  cream
1 pound cooked small
  shrimp
Paprika
Chopped parsley

With scissors, trim the ends of the artichoke leaves and discard the thorns. In a large pot, cover the artichokes with water. Add the oil. Bring to a boil and simmer about 45 minutes. When done, a leaf will pull off easily. Cool and remove leaves from the artichoke hearts.

Combine cheese, Tabasco, salt, and cream to make a smooth paste. Spread a little of the cheese paste on each artichoke leaf. Place a shrimp on top and sprinkle with paprika and chopped parsley.

Arrange the leaves on a round platter in the shape of a flower.

Four ¼-ounce envelopes
    unflavored gelatin
1 tablespoon sugar
1 teaspoon salt
1 teaspoon dry mustard
A few drops of Tabasco
    sauce
1 cup water
¼ cup freshly squeezed
    lime juice
4 cups crab meat, flaked
    (lobster meat may be
    substituted)
1 cup finely diced celery
1 cup finely diced green
    bell pepper
2 cups heavy cream,
    whipped

1 cup sour cream
1 cup heavy cream
¼ cup minced onion
Two 4-ounce jars caviar

crab mousse with caviar cream

In a small saucepan, mix the gelatin, sugar, salt, mustard, and Tabasco. Add the water and lime juice. Place over a low flame, stirring constantly until gelatin is dissolved. Chill until the mixture reaches the consistency of unbeaten egg whites. Fold in the crab meat, celery, green pepper, and whipped cream. Turn into a 10-cup ring mold and chill until firm. Unmold onto a serving platter and smooth Caviar Cream (recipe follows) over the top.

caviar cream:

Combine all ingredients, stirring gently until blended.

3 cups mayonnaise
6 hard-cooked egg yolks,
   mashed (reserve whites
   for Salad)
1 cup sweet pickle relish,
   well drained
6 drops Tabasco sauce
1 teaspoon Worcestershire
   sauce
2 tablespoons chopped
   green onion
1 tablespoon freshly
   squeezed lemon juice

salad:

2 pounds cooked boneless
   chicken breast, cut in
   ½-inch pieces
2 pounds cooked lobster
   meat, cut in ½-inch
   pieces
2 pounds cooked small
   shrimp, cut in half
6 hard-cooked egg whites,
   chopped
3 cups chopped celery
1 cup chopped red, yellow,
   and green bell peppers,
   mixed
4 cups mixed lettuce
   leaves
Chopped parsley, for
   garnish

lobster, shrimp, and chicken salad

An elegant and luscious delight to add to your guests' pleasure. A small plate and fork will be needed for this.

Combine all the dressing ingredients. Cover and chill until ready to use.

Combine the chicken, lobster, and shrimp. Stir in the chopped egg whites, celery, and peppers.

Arrange the lettuce leaves on a large platter. Mix the lobster-shrimp-chicken mixture with the dressing. Use a rubber spatula for easy mixing. Pile the salad mixture on the lettuce leaves and garnish with chopped parsley.

chocolate meringue puffs

makes approximately 30 puffs

3 egg whites
Pinch of cream of tartar
¾ cup sugar
1 teaspoon vanilla extract
2 tablespoons cocoa
⅓ cup Planters nut
   topping
1 ½ cups semisweet
   chocolate bits

Preheat oven to 300°. Grease two 10 × 15-inch cookie sheets—cover each sheet with a piece of parchment paper.

Beat the egg whites and cream of tartar until stiff. Slowly add the sugar and vanilla extract. Beat until soft peaks form. Fold in the cocoa. Gently fold in the nut topping and chocolate bits with a rubber spatula.

Drop by tablespoons onto the prepared cookie sheets. Bake until dry, 30 to 35 minutes. Peel meringues off the parchment paper.

buffet dinners

Buffet dinners allow you to create a spontaneous exchange of appetites and atmosphere. Feel free to mix the traditional with the unexpected, as long as you obey one rule: Aim for a balance of flavors, textures, and colors. Although most buffets are designed for large groups, the menus planned here are for groups of 6. Buffet entertaining is informal and gay, and more relaxing for the host or hostess than a formal sit-down dinner.

One of the advantages of buffet entertaining is that it can be as simple or elaborate as you or your guest list dictate. Entertaining in a simple yet sophisticated style is the secret of successful party planning.

An asterisk is used to indicate recipes that are not included in this book.

a holiday buffet

❖

appetizers to be passed first
checkerboard caviar tray
smoked salmon wheels

on the buffet table
rack of lamb
or
caliente roast leg of lamb with jalapeño and tequila
cabbage rolls stuffed with brown rice
hot dinner rolls*

dessert to be placed on buffet table after
main course is cleared
ginger mousse

1977 warre's port
espresso*

❖

Taittinger Brut NV and 1985 Joseph Phelps "Insignia" or 1978
Robert Mondavi Reserve Cabernet Sauvignon.

checkerboard caviar tray

Softened butter
1 package cocktail
 pumpernickel, cut in
 1 ½-inch squares
1 package cocktail toast
One 4-ounce jar black
 lump caviar
One 4-ounce jar golden or
 red lump caviar
1 cup crème fraîche❖ or
 sour cream
Lemon juice
¼ cup very finely chopped
 green onions

Spread butter on each bread square. Spread a thin layer of black caviar on the toast. Spread a thin layer of golden or red caviar on the pumpernickel. Add a dollop of crème fraîche or sour cream to each square. Sprinkle with lemon juice and chopped green onions. Arrange alternately on a square tray to resemble a checkerboard.

1 cup heavy cream
1 teaspoon buttermilk

In a bowl, mix ingredients well. Cover the bowl with a paper towel or a dish cloth. Place in a turned-off gas oven or let stand at room temperature for 10 to 12 hours. After the mixture has thickened, place in a screw-top jar and refrigerate.

❖ Crème Fraîche is available in the dairy case of specialty food shops or supermarkets. It is also easy to make and will keep under refrigeration for 10 days.

smoked salmon wheels

One 3-ounce package
 cream cheese
1 tablespoon bottled
 creamy horseradish
 sauce
¼ teaspoon chopped fresh
 dill
¼ pound smoked salmon,
 sliced
Fresh dill sprigs, for
 garnish

Mix the cream cheese, horseradish, and chopped dill together until soft. Spread on the smoked salmon slices. Roll up each slice and secure with a toothpick.
 Garnish the serving tray with sprigs of fresh dill.

rack of lamb

2 racks of rib or loin lamb
 chops (6 to 7 chops on
 each)
Salt and pepper, to taste
2 cups bread crumbs
1 teaspoon dried
 rosemary, crumbled
1 clove garlic, minced
¼ pound (1 stick) butter,
 melted

Have the butcher scrape the meat from the tips of the
bones in order to expose them. Place the racks together on
a rack in a roasting pan with bones facing and alternating
the full length of the racks.

Season the lamb with salt and pepper. In a bowl, combine the remaining ingredients. Rub and press the crumb
mixture over the lamb. Cover the tips of the bones with foil.
Roast for 10 minutes, then reduce oven temperature to
375°. Roast for an additional 25 to 30 minutes, or until
desired doneness is reached (135° on a meat thermometer
for medium rare). Remove the foil, cut between the bones,
and serve.

caliente roast leg of lamb with jalapeño and tequila

4 cloves garlic, peeled
6 fresh jalapeño peppers, coarsely chopped
½ cup gold tequila
4 teaspoons Dijon mustard
1 teaspoon salt
2 teaspoons coarsely ground pepper
One 6- to 7-pound leg of lamb, boned, rolled, and tied

🌶 sauce:

One 8-ounce jar apple mint jelly
One 8-ounce jar pineapple chutney or pineapple preserves
One 4-ounce bottle prepared white horseradish
½ teaspoon dry hot mustard

This sauce is also a good accompaniment for the Rack of Lamb.

Combine all ingredients except the lamb in a food processor. Process until well blended. Rub the entire surface of the lamb with this mixture, pressing it in with some force.

Set the lamb in a roasting pan and cover with plastic wrap. Marinate for several hours or overnight in the refrigerator.

Preheat oven to 400°. Roast the lamb, uncovered, for 30 minutes, turning to brown on all sides. Reduce the heat to 350° and continue roasting for 2½ hours, or until the lamb is very tender. Let rest for 15 to 20 minutes before carving.

Combine all ingredients and chill. Serve cold, on the side.

variation: Substitute a jar of cherry preserves for the pineapple chutney. A delicious taste treat!

cabbage rolls stuffed with brown rice

12 cabbage leaves
2 tablespoons butter
2 tablespoons finely
  chopped onion
1 fresh jalapeño pepper,
  finely chopped
1 ½ cups cooked brown
  rice
1 cup cooked peas
¼ cup golden raisins
¼ cup piñon nuts
¼ cup (½ stick) melted
  butter

Preheat oven to 350°. Plunge the cabbage leaves, a few at a time, into a large pot of boiling water. Leave in only long enough to make the leaf pliable, a few seconds. Set aside.

Melt the 2 tablespoons butter in a skillet. Sauté the onion and jalapeño until wilted. Remove from heat, add the rice, peas, raisins, and nuts. Stir to mix. Place about one tablespoon of the rice mixture on each cabbage leaf. Overlap the sides and roll up. Place the rolls seam side down in a flat pan and pour melted butter over the top. Bake until heated through, about 10 minutes.

ginger mousse

3 egg yolks
4 tablespoons dark brown
  sugar
1 teaspoon ground ginger
1 cup heavy cream
1 tablespoon crystallized
  ginger, chopped
6 gingersnap cookies,
  crushed to coarse
  crumbs

Put the egg yolks, brown sugar, and ground ginger in the top of a double boiler over simmering water. Beat with an electric mixer or rotary beater at high speed until slightly thickened.

Remove from heat and place the pan over ice water. Beat a minute or two more. In a separate bowl, whip the cream until stiff. With a rubber spatula, fold the crystallized ginger and whipped cream into the egg mixture. Divide among 6 glass dessert bowls or wine glasses and chill several hours. Garnish with gingersnap crumbs before serving.

a chinese medley

❖

appetizers
smoked oyster puffs

soup
mug of mushroom soup

buffet
chinese pork
piñon rice
snow peas with green onion

dessert
quick peach melba

coffee served with germain-robin and mendocino
alembic brandy*

❖

*Serve 1990 Cakebread Sauvignon Blanc, Napa Valley, and 1986
Guigal Côtes-du-Rhône to complement these Oriental flavors.*

smoked oyster puffs

One 8-ounce package
  cream cheese, softened
¼ cup half-and-half
2 tablespoons finely
  minced green onions,
  white part only
1 teaspoon Worcestershire
  sauce
½ teaspoon Tabasco
  sauce
1 egg yolk, beaten
One 3⅔-ounce can
  smoked oysters,
  drained
10 thinly sliced whole
  wheat bread slices

Preheat oven to 375°. Combine the softened cream cheese, the half-and-half, onion, Worcestershire, Tabasco, and egg yolk in a blender. Process until thoroughly mixed.

Remove to a bowl with a rubber spatula and gently fold in the oysters.

Cut the bread into small rounds and toast on one side. Spread the side not toasted with the oyster mixture. Arrange rounds on a cookie sheet and bake for 5 minutes, or until lightly browned and puffed. Serve hot.

mug of mushroom soup

2 tablespoons butter
1 pound fresh
  mushrooms, finely
  chopped
2 tablespoons minced
  shallot
1 tablespoon fresh minced
  jalapeño pepper
1 teaspoon salt
2 tablespoons freshly
  squeezed lemon juice
2 tablespoons flour
2 cups chicken or beef
  broth
2 cups heavy cream

Melt the butter in a 2-quart saucepan. Add the mush-rooms, shallot, jalapeño, salt, and lemon juice. Cook for about 10 minutes, stirring often. Stir in the flour. Add the broth and bring to a boil. Reduce heat, add the cream, and mix well with a wire whisk. Simmer for about 20 minutes. Taste for seasoning. Serve in mugs.

chinese pork

2 tablespoons peanut oil
2 pounds boneless pork
    loin, cut into ¾-inch
    cubes
Salt and pepper, to taste
One 8-ounce can
    pineapple chunks,
    drained, juice reserved
One 11-ounce can
    mandarin orange
    sections, drained, juice
    reserved
Water
3 tablespoons cornstarch
1 tablespoon soy sauce
2 tablespoons prepared
    mustard
2 tablespoons white
    vinegar
½ cup molasses
½ teaspoon ground ginger
1 large green bell pepper,
    diced
One 3-ounce can chow
    mein noodles
One 8-ounce can sliced
    water chestnuts,
    drained

Preheat oven to 350°. In a large skillet, heat the oil and sauté the pork cubes until brown. Sprinkle with salt and pepper and set aside. Combine the reserved fruit juices in a measuring cup and add enough water to make 2 cups. Stir in the cornstarch to thicken. Combine with the soy sauce. Stir in the mustard, vinegar, molasses, and ginger. Add to the pork. Stir to combine.

Cover and simmer slowly for 15 minutes, stirring occasionally. Add the pineapple, orange sections, and green pepper. Stir gently. Pour the mixture into a shallow 3-quart casserole and bake for 30 minutes. Sprinkle the chow mein noodles and water chestnuts over the top during the last 5 minutes of baking.

piñon rice

1 tablespoon peanut oil
1 tablespoon butter
1 green onion, chopped
1 cup uncooked white rice
¾ cup piñon nuts
2 cups water
½ teaspoon salt

In 2-quart stockpot, heat the oil and butter. Add the onion, rice, and piñon nuts. Sauté until the nuts start to change color. Add the water and salt. Cover and simmer for 20 to 25 minutes, until the rice is cooked and the water is absorbed.

snow peas with green onion

1 pound fresh snow peas
   or two 6-ounce
   packages frozen
2 tablespoons butter
1 green onion, chopped
½ teaspoon lemon pepper
Salt and pepper, to taste

Lightly steam the snow peas—be sure to not overcook. Melt the butter in a 12-inch skillet. Add the onion, steamed snow peas, and the lemon pepper. Sauté for 1 to 2 minutes. Season with salt and pepper. Serve hot.

quick peach melba

Slice peaches, fresh or canned, over a piece of sponge cake. Add a small scoop of vanilla ice cream, and top with bottled raspberry sauce.

❦ sponge cake: (available from most good bakeries, or use this easy recipe)

1 cup flour
¼ teaspoon salt
6 eggs, separated
1 cup extra-fine granulated sugar
1 tablespoon lemon juice
Grated rind of 1 lemon
Confectioners sugar

Preheat oven to 350°. Grease and lightly flour a 9 × 5 × 3-inch loaf pan. Sift together the flour and salt. In a bowl, beat the egg yolks until thick and lemon colored. In a separate bowl, beat the egg whites with an electric mixer until stiff.

Add the granulated sugar to the egg whites, 2 tablespoons at a time, beating thoroughly after each addition. Beat in the lemon juice and rind. Fold in the egg yolks with a rubber spatula. Cut and fold in the flour mixture, a small amount at a time.

Fill the prepared pan ¾ full and smooth the top. You will have some batter left over to use for cupcakes.

Bake for 30 to 35 minutes, or until the cake tests done. (Gently press your knuckles into the center of the cake. If it springs back, it's done.)

Cool in the pan for 5 minutes. Then turn the cake out onto a rack to cool completely. Sprinkle with confectioners sugar.

a southwestern vegetarian supper

This menu is perfect for a Sunday night supper party or any informal occasion, such as watching a game on TV. All the preparation can be done in advance.

❖

drinks
three-citrus margarita

soup
santa fe tortilla soup

buffet
brown rice enchiladas with goat cheese, black bean
sauce, and salsa fresca
mixed pepper salad

dessert
pumpkin mousse amaretto

coffee*

❖

*1989 Byron Pinot Noir Reserve and 1990 Wente Chardonnay
Reserve go well with this Southwestern supper.*

three – citrus margarita

1 ounce El Tesoro Plata
  tequila
1 ounce Grand Marnier
Juice of 1 fresh lime
Juice of ½ fresh lemon
Juice of ½ fresh orange

Blend all ingredients and serve over ice.

santa fe tortilla soup

3 tablespoons olive oil
1 cup roasted, peeled, and
  chopped hot green
  chilies
1 large onion, chopped
2 cloves garlic, minced
2 teaspoons New
  Mexican red chili
  powder
One 1-quart can chicken
  broth
3 large tomatoes, chopped
One 8-ounce can tomato
  sauce
1 teaspoon salt, or to
  taste
¼ teaspoon Maggi
  seasoning
Crisp tortilla chips
½ pound Monterey Jack
  cheese, shredded
Cilantro, for garnish

In a 2-quart pot, heat the olive oil and sauté the green chilies, onion, and garlic. Mix in the red chili powder and sauté, stirring, for about 5 minutes. Add the chicken broth, chopped tomatoes, tomato sauce, salt, and Maggi seasoning.

Bring to a boil. Lower heat and simmer for 45 minutes. Just before serving, place 4 or 5 tortilla chips in each of 6 ovenproof bowls. Pour soup over the chips and sprinkle with cheese. Place under the broiler to melt the cheese. Garnish each serving with a sprig of cilantro.

brown rice enchiladas with goat cheese, black bean sauce, and salsa fresca

2 cups warm cooked
   brown rice
1 cup canned garbanzo
   beans, drained
½ pound mild goat cheese
   (such as Montrachet),
   broken into small pieces
1 tablespoon chopped
   fresh jalapeño pepper
1 tablespoon chopped
   onion
½ cup sour cream
Salt, to taste
1 cup peanut oil
12 white corn tortillas
Black Bean Sauce (recipe
   follows)
1 cup shredded Monterey
   Jack cheese
Chopped lettuce, on the
   side
Chopped tomatoes, on the
   side

Preheat oven to 350°. In a large bowl, gently but thoroughly mix the rice, garbanzo beans, goat cheese, jalapeño, onion, sour cream, and salt. Set aside.

In a heavy skillet, heat the oil until very hot and dip the tortillas in it, one at a time, for about 3 seconds. The tortillas should be soft and pliable, not crisp. Drain on paper towels.

Place 3 heaping tablespoons of the rice mixture across the center of each tortilla. Roll up. Place side by side, seam side down, in a 12 × 8 × 2-inch baking dish. Spread warm Black Bean Sauce over the top and sprinkle with the Monterey Jack. Bake 15 minutes, or until the cheese is melted.

Serve bowls of chopped lettuce, chopped tomatoes, additional Black Bean Sauce and Salsa Fresca (recipes on following page) on the side for guests to garnish enchiladas as desired.

❦ black bean sauce:

2 tablespoons olive oil
1 clove garlic, chopped
¼ cup chopped onion
1 ancho chili, seeded and
    chopped
Two 16-ounce cans black
    beans, drained
2 fresh jalapeño peppers,
    chopped
Salt, to taste
One 10½-ounce can
    chicken broth
2 or 3 dashes Tabasco
    sauce

In a 2-quart saucepan, heat the oil and sauté the garlic, onion, and chili pepper until wilted. Combine with the remaining ingredients. Transfer to a food processor and process only until mixed. The sauce should be coarse in texture. Taste for seasoning. Serve warm.

❦ salsa fresca:

½ cup coarsely chopped
    red onion
½ cup coarsely chopped
    yellow onion
4 peeled ripe tomatoes,
    coarsely chopped
1 clove garlic, mashed
One 12-ounce jar pickled
    jalapeño peppers, with
    juice
¼ cup chopped parsley
Teaspoon each: cilantro,
    coriander, ground
    cumin
Salt, to taste

Combine all ingredients. Refrigerate, covered, for several hours before serving, to blend flavors.

mixed pepper salad

1 large red bell pepper,
  seeded and sliced in
  narrow strips
1 large yellow bell pepper,
  seeded and sliced in
  narrow strips
1 medium green bell
  pepper, seeded and
  sliced in narrow strips
1 cup sliced fresh
  mushrooms
1 tablespoon chopped
  fresh jalapeño pepper
1 medium red onion,
  peeled, thinly sliced,
  and separated into
  rings
1 medium-size ripe
  avocado, peeled and cut
  into bite-size pieces
Fresh lime wedges, for
  garnish

🌿 dressing:

¾ cup olive oil
¼ cup balsamic vinegar
1 teaspoon Dijon mustard
¼ teaspoon salt
Dash of black pepper
Pinch of sugar

Make this salad several hours before it is to be served, or even the day before. But don't add the avocado until just before serving.

In a large bowl combine all ingredients except the avocado and lime. Prepare the dressing.

Combine all ingredients in a screw-top jar and shake to blend. Over the pepper and mushroom mixture, pour only as much as is needed to moisten. Toss and refrigerate overnight, or for several hours.

At serving time, peel and cut the avocado. Gently mix with the peppers. Serve in a shallow bowl and garnish with wedges of fresh lime.

pumpkin mousse amaretto

One ¼-ounce envelope
  unflavored gelatin
¼ cup cold water
½ cup Amaretto liqueur
½ cup sugar
1 tablespoon freshly
  squeezed lemon juice
1 teaspoon ground ginger
One 16-ounce can
  mashed pumpkin
1 cup sour cream
1 cup heavy cream,
  whipped
Sweetened Whipped
  Cream, for garnish
  (recipe follows)
Chopped walnuts, for
  garnish

The tantalizing flavor of this almond liqueur combined with the pumpkin, produces an extremely elegant and magic dessert.

Soften the gelatin in the cold water. Dissolve over hot water or in a microwave. Add the Amaretto, sugar, lemon juice, and ginger. Stir and blend well. Chill until slightly thickened.

Mix the pumpkin with the sour cream and whipped cream. Fold into the gelatin mixture and blend well. Turn into a 6-cup greased ring mold and chill until firm.

Unmold onto a serving platter and garnish with Sweetened Whipped Cream and walnuts.

❧ sweetened whipped cream:

½ cup heavy cream,
  whipped
1 to 2 tablespoons sugar
1 to 2 tablespoons vanilla
  extract

Fold sugar and vanilla into whipped cream.

variation: Chocolate—Add 1 tablespoon cocoa.
Lemon—Add 1 teaspoon fresh lemon juice in place of the vanilla
Peppermint—Add ½ teaspoon peppermint extract in place of vanilla

a classic steamed chicken and vegetable dinner

For a perfect simple dinner, without a chili or jalapeño pepper in sight, try this pleasing and delectable menu. Cooking in steam is a lovely and efficient way to produce beautiful, healthful, and wonderful-tasting food. Most kitchens today are equipped with steamers—electric or otherwise—and many kitchens have bamboo baskets to stack over a wok so that an entire meal can be cooked simultaneously.

❖

appetizer
crab and water chestnuts on toast

buffet
breast of chicken with fresh peas and
mushroom sauce
new potatoes with butter and chives
nutty orange muffins

dessert
banana pudding parfait with chocolate
whipped cream

coffee *or* espresso*
kir*

❖

1990 Meridian Edna Valley Chardonnay and 1987
Jordan Cabernet Sauvignon are perfect accompaniments to this
perfectly simple meal.

crab and water chestnuts on toast

2 cups cooked, shredded crab meat, cartilage removed

One 8-ounce can water chestnuts, drained and chopped

1 tablespoon finely chopped green onion, white part only

1 teaspoon soy sauce

½ cup mayonnaise

1 box cocktail toast squares

Chopped parsley, for garnish

Make this spread several hours before dinner.

Combine all ingredients except the toast and parsley. Cover and chill. Spread the crab mixture on toast and garnish with chopped parsley just before serving.

breast of chicken with fresh peas and mushroom sauce

1 cup white wine

½ teaspoon crushed garlic

1 teaspoon salt

2 tablespoons chopped parsley

½ teaspoon savory

½ teaspoon sweet basil

¼ teaspoon pepper

3 boneless chicken breasts, cut in half (2 to 2 ½ pounds total)

1 ½ cups shelled fresh peas

⚘ mushroom sauce:

3 tablespoons butter

2 tablespoons finely chopped shallots

1 ½ cups sliced fresh mushrooms

Reserved chicken marinade

¾ cup heavy cream

1 tablespoon cornstarch

3 tablespoons cold water

Combine the wine, garlic, salt, parsley, savory, basil, and pepper in a shallow baking dish. Add the chicken breasts and marinate 30 minutes or more.

When ready to steam, heat water in bottom of a steamer. Remove the chicken, reserving the marinade, and place in the top of the steamer with the peas. Cover and steam for 15 minutes.

While steaming, prepare the Mushroom Sauce.

In a skillet, heat the butter, add the shallots and mushrooms, and sauté for 5 minutes. Add the reserved marinade and heat to boiling. Reduce heat, add the cream, and cook 2 or 3 minutes, until thickened.

Mix the cornstarch with the cold water and add to the sauce. Stir quickly, until thickened and remove from heat.

Arrange the chicken and peas on a platter and cover with the sauce. Serve at once.

new potatoes with butter and chives

6 to 10 unpeeled new
   potatoes, cut into
   ¼-inch slices
½ cup butter
Salt and pepper, to taste
5 tablespoons chopped
   fresh chives

Fill the bottom of a steamer with water. Heat to boiling. Reduce heat and put potato slices in the top of the steamer. Cover and cook 10 to 15 minutes, or until tender. Do not overcook. Heat the butter in a small saucepan. Remove the potatoes to a serving bowl. Season with salt and pepper, toss with the melted butter, and sprinkle with chives. Serve immediately.

nutty orange muffins

2 cups flour
1 teaspoon baking soda
1 teaspoon salt
2 tablespoons sugar
½ cup vegetable
   shortening (Crisco)
2 tablespoons grated
   orange rind
¾ cup chopped pecans
1 egg, beaten
1 ¼ cups buttermilk

Preheat oven to 450°. Sift the flour, soda, and salt together. Add the sugar and cut in the shortening until mixture is the consistency of cornmeal. Add the orange rind and nuts. Fold in the egg and buttermilk to make a soft dough.

   Fill 12 greased muffin cups ¾ full. Bake about 15 minutes.

banana pudding parfait with chocolate whipped cream

½ cup sugar
2 eggs
¼ cup flour
2 cups half-and-half, scalded
½ cup butter
1 teaspoon vanilla extract
5 medium-size ripe bananas, peeled and sliced
6 vanilla wafers, coarsely crumbled
Chocolate Whipped Cream (recipe follows)

In a heavy saucepan, beat the sugar, eggs, and flour until lemon colored. Slowly add the scalded half-and-half to the egg mixture. Cook, stirring constantly, until the sauce thickens, about 5 minutes. Remove from the heat and fold in the butter and vanilla. Transfer the custard to a bowl, cover with plastic wrap, and cool in the refrigerator. Just before serving, fold in the bananas, reserving 6 pieces for garnish.

In each of 6 chilled parfait glasses, alternate layers of vanilla wafer crumbs with custard. Top each parfait with Chocolate Whipped Cream and a banana slice.

❧ chocolate whipped cream:

1 cup heavy cream
1 teaspoon cocoa
1 teaspoon sugar

Whip the cream until stiff. Gently fold in the cocoa and sugar.

olio buffet

❖

appetizer
deviled seafood au gratin
in scallop shells

buffet
honey-glazed chicken breasts
or
sunshine chicken breasts
sautéed spinach
chinese brown rice
jalapeño-pecan cornbread

dessert
butterscotch parfait

coffee

a. e. dor vsop cognac

❖

*To complement the Olio Buffet, serve 1990 Markham Sauvignon
Blanc and 1988 Acacia Pinot Noir "Carneros."*

deviled seafood au gratin in scallop shells

1 cup Heinz chili sauce
1 cup cooked and coarsely
   shredded crab meat
12 cooked shrimp
12 raw oysters
Lemon juice
1 teaspoon Worcestershire
   sauce
1 teaspoon minced fresh
   jalapeño pepper
1 teaspoon minced green
   bell pepper
2 slices bacon, cooked
   crisp and crumbled
Freshly grated Parmesan
   cheese

You will need six scallop-shaped baking shells.*

Preheat oven to 400°. Place 1 tablespoon of chili sauce in each baking shell. Divide the crab meat on top of the sauce. Place 2 shrimp and 2 oysters in each shell. Sprinkle with lemon juice.

Combine the Worcestershire sauce, jalapeño, and green pepper with the remaining chili sauce and pour over the seafood. Sprinkle with bacon and Parmesan cheese.

Bake 10 minutes, until hot.

❖ These shells are available in kitchen supply and gourmet shops.

honey-glazed chicken breasts

1 small onion
1 carrot, thinly sliced
1 celery stalk, thinly sliced
2 sprigs parsley
1 teaspoon salt
½ teaspoon pepper
1 small bay leaf
One 14½-ounce can
  chicken broth
1 cup water
Six 10- to 12-ounce
  chicken breasts,
  skinned, boned, and
  cut in half
½ cup honey
Seedless grapes and
  watercress, for garnish
½ cup toasted sliced
  almonds

In a 6-quart saucepan, combine the onion, carrot, celery, parsley, salt, pepper, bay leaf, chicken broth, and water. Bring to a boil and add the chicken breasts. Lower the heat, cover, and simmer for 20 to 25 minutes, until chicken is tender.

Remove from heat and cool the chicken in the broth, then place the saucepan in the refrigerator overnight.

Next day, remove the chicken from the broth and place in a shallow baking pan. Add 1 cup broth to the pan. (Strain the remaining broth and freeze for future use in soups or stews.)

Preheat the broiler. Brush the breasts with half the honey and broil for 2 minutes. Brush with the remaining honey and continue broiling for 2 more minutes, or until the chicken is brown and glazed.

Transfer the chicken to a large serving platter and garnish with grapes and watercress. Sprinkle with the almonds and serve immediately.

sunshine chicken breasts

6 skinless half chicken
   breasts or 3 whole
   breasts, split in half
   and skinned
   (3 pounds, total)
1 ½ teaspoons curry
   powder
½ teaspoon dry mustard
2 tablespoons honey
1 teaspoon grated orange
   rind
½ cup freshly squeezed
   orange juice
½ teaspoon salt
¼ teaspoon pepper
2 or 3 oranges, peeled and
   sliced
Parsley, for garnish

Preheat oven to 350°. Rub the chicken breasts with the curry powder and mustard. Press well into the flesh. Place in an 11 × 7½ × 2-inch baking dish. Combine the honey, orange rind, juice, salt, and pepper and pour over the chicken. Cover the dish tightly with aluminum foil and bake for 35 to 40 minutes.

Turn the chicken, baste with the pan juices, re-cover with foil, and bake an additional 15 minutes, or until the chicken is tender.

Arrange the chicken breasts on a platter and pour the liquid over them. Surround with the orange slices and garnish with parsley.

sautéed spinach

⅓ cup olive oil
1 ½ pounds fresh
   spinach, washed, dried,
   and chopped
½ cup chicken broth
½ teaspoon salt
½ teaspoon pepper
Dash of nutmeg

Heat the oil in a skillet over medium heat. Add the spinach, a handful at a time, adding more as it wilts. Add the chicken broth and sauté for about 2 minutes. Season with salt, pepper, and nutmeg.

chinese brown rice

½ cup oil (sesame oil combined with 2 tablespoons hot oil)
¾ cup thinly sliced green bell pepper
¾ cup thinly sliced celery
½ cup slivered almonds
6 cups cooked brown rice
One 8-ounce can water chestnuts, drained and sliced
6 large dried mushrooms, soaked and sliced
1 tablespoon soy sauce, or to taste

Heat ¼ cup of the oil in a large skillet or wok. Add the green pepper, celery, and almonds. Stir constantly until the almonds are lightly browned. Remove from the pan and set aside.

In the same pan, heat the remaining oil and add the rice. Stir constantly until the rice is well coated. Stir in the water chestnuts and mushrooms. Add the green pepper mixture and the soy sauce. Stir until the rice is heated through.

jalapeño - pecan cornbread

2 ½ cups yellow cornmeal
1 cup flour
2 tablespoons sugar
1 teaspoon salt
4 teaspoons baking powder
6 to 8 jalapeño peppers, chopped
1 ½ cups milk
3 eggs
½ cup vegetable oil
One 7-ounce can cream-style corn
1 cup broken pecan pieces
1 cup shredded sharp Cheddar cheese

Preheat oven to 400°. Grease two 9 × 11-inch baking pans. Mix together the cornmeal, flour, sugar, salt, baking powder, and jalapeño. Stir in the remaining ingredients. Spoon the mixture into the prepared pans. Bake for 20 to 25 minutes.

7/4/99 was a little dry. Try using only one pan and/or the full 14oz. can of creamed corn

butterscotch parfait

1 quart vanilla ice cream
One 12-ounce jar butterscotch topping
1 cup whipped cream
½ cup chopped nuts (pecans, walnuts, or almonds)

In 6 parfait or 7-ounce wine glasses, layer vanilla ice cream with butterscotch topping. Place in the freezer until 5 or 10 minutes before serving. Top with a spoonful of whipped cream and sprinkle with chopped nuts.

a fish story

❖

appetizer
salmon patties with cucumber sauce
gruet brut champagne

buffet
southwest stuffed trout with jalapeño-lime
mayonnaise
vegetable platter
hot rolls*

dessert
strawberry-banana whimsy

coffee and brandy*

❖

Serve 1988 Sonoma-Cutrer Chardonnay *"Les Pierres"* and 1989
Caymus Zinfandel with the fish buffet.

One 16-ounce can red
    sockeye salmon
1 cup fine cracker crumbs,
    plus 1 cup cracker
    crumbs for coating
    patties
1 teaspoon minced green
    onion
1 tablespoon chopped
    parsley
1 teaspoon Worcestershire
    sauce
½ teaspoon Tabasco
    sauce
1 egg
2 tablespoons mayonnaise
2 tablespoons butter
1 tablespoon olive oil
Chopped parsley, for
    garnish
Lemon wedges, for
    garnish

salmon patties with cucumber sauce

Drain the salmon and flake into a bowl with 1 cup of cracker crumbs, the onion, parsley, Worcestershire, Tabasco, egg, and mayonnaise. Shape into 6 patties. Coat each patty lightly with the remaining cracker crumbs.

Heat the butter and olive oil in a large skillet and fry the patties, turning them to brown on both sides. Add more butter, if necessary.

Transfer to a serving platter, sprinkle with chopped parsley, and surround with lemon wedges. Serve with Cucumber Sauce (recipe follows).

2 cups peeled, finely
    chopped and drained
    cucumber
1 cup mayonnaise
1 cup sour cream
½ teaspoon grated onion
½ teaspoon crumbled dill
    weed
1 tablespoon lemon juice
Salt and pepper, to taste

❧ cucumber sauce:

Combine all ingredients and mix well. Chill before serving.

6 whole trout (rainbow or
  Rocky Mountain),
  cleaned and boned
3 slices bacon, diced
½ cup minced onion
¼ cup minced fresh green
  chilies
1 ½ cups fresh bread
  crumbs
One 8-ounce can whole-
  kernel corn
1 egg
½ teaspoon salt
¼ teaspoon pepper
3 slices bacon, cut in half

southwest stuffed trout with jalapeño - lime mayonnaise

Preheat oven to 375°. To make the stuffing, cook the diced bacon until brown. Remove the bacon from the pan and add the onion and green chilies to the drippings. Sauté briefly. Stir in the bread crumbs, corn, egg, salt, pepper, and cooked bacon.

Stuff the trout with this mixture. Place the stuffed trout in a pan and top each one with a half slice of bacon. Bake 30 minutes. Serve with Jalapeño-Lime Mayonnaise (recipe follows) on the side.

✎ jalapeño-lime mayonnaise:

2 cups mayonnaise
1 fresh jalapeño pepper,
  finely chopped
3 to 4 tablespoons freshly
  squeezed lime juice

Combine all ingredients and chill until ready to serve.

vegetable platter

6 small unpeeled new
    potatoes
One 10-ounce package
    frozen sliced string
    beans
1 red bell pepper, seeded
    and cut into strips
1 yellow bell pepper,
    seeded and cut into
    strips
12 asparagus spears,
    steamed or parboiled
1 large ripe avocado,
    sliced

❧ dressing:

¼ cup balsamic vinegar
½ teaspoon Dijon
    mustard
1 teaspoon honey
Salt, to taste
¾ cup olive oil

Drop the potatoes in boiling water to cover. Cook 10 to 15 minutes; test for doneness, drain, and, when cool, cut in half. Cook the beans according to package directions.

Arrange the vegetables in separate rows on a serving platter. Combine the vinegar, mustard, honey, and salt for the dressing in a screw-top jar and shake until well mixed. Add the oil and shake again. Sprinkle over the vegetables.

strawberry-banana whimsy

1 cup sugar
¾ cup water
1 tablespoon cornstarch
¼ cup cold water
1 pint strawberries, hulled
  and sliced in half
2 bananas, thinly sliced
1 tablespoon lemon juice
½ cup toasted slivered
  almonds
1 cup heavy cream,
  whipped

Bring the sugar and water to a boil. Blend the cornstarch with the cold water and add to the sugar water. Stir until thickened. Combine the strawberries and bananas in a bowl with the lemon juice. Pour the cooked sauce over the fruit. Cool and chill.

Serve in glass bowls or wine glasses, sprinkled with almonds and topped with whipped cream.

index